Don't Think Of A Republican

How I Won A Republican Primary As A Lefty Progressive And You Can Too

H.F. Valentine

Don't Think Of A Republican
How I Won A Republican Primary As A Lefty Progressive
And You Can Too
H.F. Valentine
(2021, 2022, 2023)

Don't Think Of A Republican
A Proposal For Progressives (Particularly Those In The DSA)
Lonnie Ray Atkinson
(original essay - first published on Znet)

ISBN 979-8-9855830-0-7
UnsafeWords
a division of UnsafeMedia
unsafemedia.com

Contents

The following piece was published on Znet in 2021.

Don't Think Of A Republican: A Proposal For Progressives (Particularly Those In The DSA)

Throughout the 2022 primary season, I want you to explore with me the absolutely bonkers idea of running a progressive, dare I say radical, Lefty McLefterson candidate in a Republican primary in a GOP stronghold district. A kind of political thought experiment/shadow campaign, asking the question: How *exactly* would you sell progressive policies, in our current electoral climate, to an audience whose political DNA is dead set against those policies?

And, yes, I literally mean you - running as a Republican. The goal of said project is to persuade people to run. To make a case for why this idea, as cheeky as it may sound, is not really all that bonkers.

To that end, consider this piece not merely an introduction, but a call to action.

During the 2020 primaries, I was watching the Justice Democrats navigate their particular races, and I got to thinking about how many dozens and dozens of districts there are throughout the country in which, even if you won the Democratic primary as a serious progressive candidate, even if you could successfully maneuver past the dirty money and even dirtier tricks of the establishment Democrats, it just wouldn't matter because those districts have either been gerrymandered into the GOP ground or are legitimately too Republican-identifying to ever elect a Democrat. Then I thought about how many people there are out there living in those districts, whose political, economic, or social vision would be categorized as being on the left, who would actually love to run but see no point. And I thought that was a shame.

That's when it hit me. If they could just win the Republican primary, the general election would be a breeze.

And as I sat there laughing at the absurd prospect of some lefty progressive running and winning as a Republican, I started to see that that wasn't what was actually absurd.

What was absurd was the assumption, mine and apparently everyone else's, that a huge portion of the population would never vote for a candidate in the primary who offered policies they knew could improve their lives but would conflict with the Party's image. That a candidate with serious and detailed proposals for better healthcare, education, wages, infrastructure, air, water, etc. wouldn't have a chance against the Party bosses because the Party bosses would simply forbid Republican voters from supporting those policies. That people would, in the end, put party over country, put party over family, if that's what the Party told them to do.

But is that really true? I know plenty of Republicans who, when asked alone, prefer many left policies. The snag is that when they walk in the voting booth, they walk in as Republicans. And although I think it's a shame so many of our political identities currently seem to be so rigid, I started to wonder. What would be the greater challenge? To change people's party preference; in other words, to get members of the GOP base to switch over to voting Democrat. Or to allow them to keep their loyalty to the Republican Party but still be able to vote for these particular policies.

I personally believe it would be more difficult to persuade tens of thousands of die-hard Republicans to magically paint their district Blue than it would be to offer them a candidate whose policy platform was truly progressive, but would still let them say that they voted for a Republican, and to know that if that candidate were to win the primary and the general, they could still be proud their district elected a Republican.

Now, I'm sure my fellow lefties might find all kinds of wrong with that kind of thinking. And that's ok. I also believe there's much to be critical of concerning this type of allegiance. But that's not really the question. The question is: What matters the most? Party affiliation or the policies being proposed? If you had an elected Republican politician proposing policies so progressive they put Democratic leadership to shame, would it matter that that politician was a Republican?

Seriously, who gives a shit? If it's an extra vote towards modernizing our healthcare system or rescuing us from the worst of Climate Change, does it really matter whether there's an R or a D next to their name? Because, remember, the districts I'm talking about are already solidly Red districts. They're going to produce Republican Representatives anyway. Wouldn't you at least want the votes and support on progressive bills?

Furthermore, we can spend all day critiquing the mindset of Republican loyalty, but maybe it's not just about them. Maybe it's about us. Why does the Left cede half of the population to the Republicans? Are we not giving into the same label-defining-your-identity nonsense that we so often ridicule? Why do progressives allow gerrymandering to dictate whom we reach out to, as if conservatives don't deserve the same policy offerings?

And then I thought, "Lonnie, you're making it too complicated." The real question is: Why not? Why not run a progressive in the Republican primary? Conservatives have been running and winning in the Democratic Party for decades. So why not try it the other way? The worst that can happen is you lose, which you would have lost running a Democrat in these types of districts anyway. On the other hand, even if you do lose, can we imagine some real gains that might be made by the mere act of running such a campaign?

Now, I know what a lot of you are already thinking. You're thinking, "But, Lonnie, the real action is not in the Congress; it's in the streets." If the people I'm trying to get to run have such a passion for affecting change, they could just invest themselves into activism or organizing. To which, I would reply, "No shit."

That's the hidden beauty of such an endeavor. Obviously, a campaign like this would be seen to many as a stunt. And, in a way, it is. If you look at the odds related to the conventional wisdom, this does not have a huge chance of winning. But the act itself, or the stunt if you must, may offer, outside the final tally of ballots, a tremendous amount of value to activists and organizers.

Though before I explain what that value is, I should underscore that the Left has a problem in not wanting to organize, or in some cases even speak to, those on the right. But we gotta be honest with ourselves. If we're serious about ever seeing enough real structural transformation in this country to make the kind of positive change we believe is possible, it's going to take a whole lot more support than what we've got on the left. In fact, if we're truly forward thinking in our vision, it'll take far more than the entirety of the Democratic Party. It's going to take the affirmation and participation of a whole lot of those folks whom we rarely ever try to organize, speak to, or even try to understand on any level that could be considered sincere.

Indeed, if you prefer to work within the hallmark of activism, think of this as a form of extreme nonviolent protest. If we're going to actually reach those who identify as Republicans, we're going to have to meet them where they are. And a whole lot of them are at a place that will, more times than not, see our street protests as riots and see the taking of a knee as un-American. So I say, why not do the most American thing you can possibly do, and run for office?

Think of it as subversive resistance to the ideological labels that imprison us. To deconstruct the political identity assigned us by our party labels, and allow people to step outside this frame and ask questions they wouldn't normally find themselves asking, would go a long way toward changing the prevailing narrative. Which could offer an opening for future organizing, making way for unprecedented political action.

Besides, the Right has been stealing Democrats for years. It's silly to hear us going on and on about how we don't even want to talk to Republicans. I'm not saying we gotta get matching tattoos or get our pictures taken at Olan Mills together. I'm saying that for these people to take us seriously, we have to take them seriously. If we want them to listen to us, we're going to have to listen to them. For them to see us as something other than an enemy, we have to show them some genuine love and respect. And if we do that, I believe it's not a matter of even changing their minds. But rather getting them to acknowledge what they already know to be true and right, and then act on it.

If you want to change the conversation, you've got to have a conversation. And by running in the Republican primary, I believe you have a better chance at garnering the benefit of the doubt. Whereas, if you *can* garner real benefit of the doubt, win or lose, you have a shot at impacting the national discussion in a way that wouldn't happen otherwise. And, on a local level, you will have introduced yourself and the people who work on your campaign as something far from the bogeyman they might have expected before such a campaign. And they may just be willing to listen to what you have to say after the campaign as well.

Then again, forget all that. I don't want you to run just so you can build up some street cred. I don't want you to run just so you can contribute to the discussion. I want you to run to win. RUN TO WIN!

And just to make sure we're all on the same page, I'm talking about running for national office. I'm talking the United States House of Representatives. Or hell, if a Senate seat comes open, why not throw your hat in the ring? The higher profile the office, the more value in running, even if the odds are totally against you.

And no, I'm not talking about trying to just win over moderate Republicans or self-described Independents who normally vote for the GOP. I'm talking about going after the hardcore. The actual GOP base. Going after the moderates is the futile project of Chuck Schumer and Nancy Pelosi. I, on the other hand, want the hearts and minds of voters who might offer the left-leaning candidate knocking on their door directions to the nearest insane asylum. For if you can solve that part of the puzzle, the moderate pieces should fall into place.

And lastly, I'm not talking about winning these voters over with milquetoast, middle of the road, establishment Democratic nothing-burgers. I'm talking about policies that matter, progressive change that would make a fundamental difference in people's lives.

Malcolm X said, "If you stick a knife in my back nine inches and pull it out six inches, there's no progress. If you pull it all the way out, that's not progress. Progress is healing the wound that the blow made." And then he added, "They won't even admit the knife is there."

I'm embarking on this admittedly strange project because so many in the political class, on so many important issues, won't even admit the knife is there. But the knife is there. And if we're ever going to get to a place of real healing, it's going to take some bold-ass action, some audacious-ass thinking. And what I'm advocating for in this project is just one of such actions.

Now, I can imagine some of you are reading this, thinking, "Then why in the hell don't you run? If you think this is such a good idea, and you're so passionate about this stuff, why don't you take a shot at it yourself?"

The answer being, at this point in my life, I have no interest in being in Congress. And I believe that if you're going to run, you should be prepared to win *and* be excited about doing the work.

On the other hand, what I *would like* is to assist the first group of people courageous enough to take me up on this proposal, and help *them* to win. In the spirit of being transparent, I don't want to just inspire such a run. I want to be your speechwriter, or your campaign strategist. I want to make a job for myself inside a campaign that doesn't yet exist. Consider this piece (and the subsequent project) proactive sweat equity towards your historical victory.

Accordingly, I don't particularly like describing this shadow campaign as fictional. In my eyes, it just hasn't happened yet. Sure, the example I plan to offer may be satirical, but it is an example nonetheless. One meant to inspire not just someone to run, but a whole lot of someones.

One candidate is a novelty. Multiple candidates is a phenomenon.

If I could spell out my dream scenario for this shadow campaign, it would be to inspire 100 candidates to run, or at least enough to give it a name and get that name in the media consciousness as not just a coincidence and not just a trend, but an organized block. The beginning of a movement. For, once you're seen as a movement, the corporate media can no longer ignore you. And, at the very least, you know progressive media outlets will be all over you. Which may not get you voters, but will get you small dollar donations. All of which is to say, the more who run, the better it is for everyone. And if enough people run, you have a real chance of finding fire and igniting a zeitgeist.

If you're someone who, victim to political geography, may feel as if you do not have an electoral existence, someone who's already on board with these types of policies but lives in a district that is fifty shades of red, I implore you to take that regrettable reality and use it. Use it to illuminate just how little freedom is offered by our political parties. Use it to command attention for a campaign like no one has ever seen.

To my knowledge, no one has tried anything like this or even called for it. With all that could be gained no matter the final ballot count, and with all that is so fucked in our current electoral system, it's hard not to ask: Why not?

What do we really have to lose?

Lonnie Ray Atkinson

Foreword by Lonnie Ray Atkinson

The following is an excerpt from a campaign speech given at the Neely Schuster Cultural Center in January 2022. (Note: During this part of the speech, the candidate took the microphone, hopped down off the stage, and stood up on an empty seat, delivering the rest of his message smackdab in the middle of his audience.)

...You know the reason they say my candidacy is a novelty, why they say I can't possibly be serious in my run for office? It's because I'm not following the script.

It's like they've sat down to watch the same play, every two years, for their whole lives, but this time one of the characters is executing completely different lines. And they just don't know what to do with that.

Now, my question to them is, "Do you even know what play it is you're watching?"

That somehow a candidate who speaks like a regular person is not a serious candidate. That somehow a candidate who is willing to engage voters in honest and vulnerable conversations is not a serious candidate. That any candidate who would ignore the conventional wisdom of the Campaign Consultant Industrial Complex, who would ignore the tisk tisk tisk of the media gatekeepers and the punditocracy, anyone who would ignore the very narrow path laid out for candidates by the donor class. That somehow a candidate like that is the outlier, is the novelty, is the candidate who cannot possibly be serious.

If the part I'm playing doesn't even make sense to you, then what does it say about the other characters in the play, what does it say about the script, what does it say about the theater they've expected voters to sit in and quietly follow along and applaud at the end their whole lives?

I can assure you. My candidacy is serious. It is the status quo that is not serious. And it is not serious because it is not sustainable.

So to hell with their script. I ain't reciting it. To hell with their costume. I ain't wearing it. And to hell with the tiny section of the stage allotted the spotlight. I'm not standing there.

I'm standing right here. With you. Out in the audience. And I'm asking you. Do you think the show you've been watching your whole life is serious? This political theater where candidates tell you one thing on the campaign trail and then forget you even exist the morning after the election. This he-said/she-said bullshit in the media, like they don't even care what the facts actually are, what the truth actually is. This system where politicians are legally allowed to take bribes from the same interests you need legislation to protect you from. Do you think *that* is serious? Do you think that is ok, that that should be the norm?

And if you don't think that's ok, if you don't think that should be the norm, what kind of a campaign would *you* prefer? What kind of candidate would *you* actually take serious?

What show - would you like to see - in Washington DC?

Tell me now!...

***

Imagine that. Imagine a candidate saying that. Better yet, imagine a lefty progressive saying that as a candidate in a Republican primary.

If you didn't know any better, it might sound like satire. To hear those words being belted out, in an unabashed Southern drawl, by an orator commanding the crowd the way only a Hellfire and Brimstone preacher could. Except that wasn't a sermon. It was a campaign speech, given by H.F. Valentine, in his 2022 run for the U.S. House of Representatives. A candidate who, despite championing policies as progressive as any of Bernie Sanders, or as he would say, *because* he was championing such policies, would go on to win that GOP primary. Upon which, due in no small part to the solidly red Republican predisposition of said district, candidate Valentine handily won the general election and set forth to turn shit completely upside down in the U.S. Congress.

I mean it when I say it's something I really didn't see coming, even though it was technically my idea. The only credit I can take is that I beat H.F. to the punch, yet not by much. He may dispute that's where he was already headed, but I don't buy it. He was ready for this in a way that I wasn't.

I wrote the piece for Znet, not really thinking anyone would respond. My plan was to do a podcast called Don't Think Of A Republican. A limited series that would serve as a kind of shadow primary, where I merely imagined what this kind of a run would look like.

About a month before I was to start recording, H.F. contacted me and turned my what if into a what now. I immediately joined the campaign and spent the primary season watching something unfold that made my initial podcast ideas look small.

This book will no doubt serve as a case study for those who watched H.F. win and are now thinking of giving it their own shot. I asked to write this foreword because I believe it can be so much more than that.

As you read these pages, I want you to imagine. What if this could happen, again? And again? What are the implications of this spreading?

Certainly, progressive readers might be a tad interested and/or invested in the potential of such an experiment multiplying. If you support the reality of Justice Democrats, then why not the concept of Don't-Think-Of-A-Republican Republicans (similar policies but with a much meaner streak)? To see districts that have already been gerrymandered to look like a Republican Rorschach Test produce politicians with the most progressive proposals in the Congress would be quite a hoot, to say the least.

Aside from progressives though, I believe this work should be quite appealing to mainstream Republican voters across the nation. Voters who are also disgusted with the corruption in both political parties, voters who would also love to have someone fighting a real fight for their wages, their healthcare, their children's education, and all that encompasses a better future. But someone who is sincere, and not leashed to the highest campaign bidders.

Not only do I believe they would just as much enjoy imagining how such a primary might unfold in their own district, I think they would appreciate having a serious lefty speak about the interests of Republican voters in a delivery that doesn't disparage them or condescend to them. To read the words of someone championing progressive issues and then measure the values espoused with their own.

Mostly, though, I believe they would appreciate a place where they can feel it's ok to wonder about things being different. To examine their own political identity and contrast what they would actually like to see on a ballot versus the identity laid out for them by the current iteration of the Republican Party. A place to wonder, if, outside of this manufactured identity, outside of donor money, could these policies be their policies? And could they imagine casting their vote for such a candidate?

The next group I believe this book serves to benefit are those who've committed to working for positive change outside of the ballot box. Activists who could use a real breakthrough in amplifying their message. Organizers who are at least curious about the potential Easter eggs that might be hidden in such a strategy.

And to those who believe this idea was complete lunacy from the start, and that H.F. should have never run, I would still urge you to stick around. If nothing else, you can appreciate the novelty of it all. Who knows? Maybe by the end you'll have a change of heart. Or, at the very least, you will have gotten in some damn good rage reading.

For whatever reason you open these pages, one thing you need to know is that H.F. didn't run for fun. He might have made it look fun, and he definitely made it look easy. But I was there. His decision to chart such an unconventional path, and to keep going when things got really scary, was not easy. It required a supremely stubborn optimism and hell of a lot of courage.

He took every punch that was thrown at him because he really believed he could win, and because he's not fucking around when it comes to these issues. He truly wants each and every one of us, regardless of our political predilections, to get to a better place. My hope for this book is that his courage (and the conviction of his words) will inspire courage in others to begin envisioning what could have only been conjured, before the candidacy of H.F. Valentine, as a figment of aspirational satire.

Introduction by H.F. Valentine

If there's one thing I knew about Republicans, going into all this, it's that they don't like to be talked down to by someone with a fancy title, especially someone with a fancy title on the left.

Lucky for me, I didn't have any fancy titles. Before this election, I was just some dude. Like most of you, I was just trying to work my day job, help feed my family, and wait for music *that I like* to come back on the radio. There was nothing special about me. And I sure as hell didn't believe that I was better than anyone else.

In fact, it was my very un-special nature that led me to believe the task ahead was not impossible. I did not always hold these views, and on certain issues, some very serious, I had done a complete 180. Not because I had an epiphany, or because I woke up one morning wiser than thou. I just got to a place where I was able to ask questions I hadn't been willing to ask before.

So when I hear certain liberals and leftists talk about how they can't be bothered to talk to the other side, I tend to think they're being shortsighted. I knew this kind of change was possible; I knew it was a matter of questions that led me to a different place. And if there was to be one guiding principle for such a campaign, I wanted my candidacy to provide an opening for those types of questions. Not from a place of pretense or presumption, but from a place of sharing.

You don't have to have a PhD or some string of professional prefixes or suffixes to understand what is really going on in Washington DC. And you definitely don't need a pundit, a pollster, or a politician to tell you what's going on in your life. What you do need is to be comfortable asking questions. Coincidentally, I was just the Southern, working class, straight, white male to *make* Republicans comfortable.

This book is composed of selected excerpts from my interviews, videos, and stump speeches, each with a supplementary note elaborating on why I said what I said. Compared alongside the average primary race, I believe this work will lay bare how pathetically phony our usual excuse for a political contest is and how a run like this was so long overdue.

As the pages turn, I want you to contemplate how you yourself could contribute, whether by actually running or lending whatever support you can spare, to this style of campaign.

It's why I settled on transcripts rather than some quirky political memoir. However fun it would have been to write about the weirdest thing I ate at a county fair or the time a lawyer for an unnamed, wealthy tech giant unsuccessfully approached me with a horrifically lucrative offer to quietly exit the race (that shit actually happened), I'd much rather leave all that as incentive for you to find out on your own.

However wide a net my publishers may throw in the marketing of this book, my target audience is the audience I have to create. Those who would actually consider such a run for office, and anyone else who would consider working on such a campaign.

But in order for that to happen, you can't just read this nodding your head or shaking your head. I want this to be an active read. I want you to ask what kinds of questions could be raised that are never raised in a normal political race. I want you to consider all the advances we could set in motion simply by running. I want you to conceive the path, however narrow, to pulling off such a feat.

My campaign is by no means a blueprint for your own run. I don't expect you to agree with me on every position or issue. And I definitely don't want you to parrot my thinking. I want you to think for yourself, with this book serving as an inspirational taste of the tactics and rhetoric that a badass candidate *like yourself* might find your way to employing.

I want you to read it as if you're watching your own campaign unfold publicly, thinking about how you might do things, similarly or differently, in your own historical upset.

With that said, for those who didn't follow my primary, there are a couple things you should know going forward.

Because I speak like everyday people speak, there's going to be some cursing. Depending on the subject matter and how fired up I got, there may be a lot of cursing. If that is something that bothers you, I ask in advance for your forgiveness and invite you to loosen the fuck up. The point of this electoral exercise was to do away with political niceties and put voters outside the mindset of establishment etiquette.

Secondly, before anyone either gets their feelings hurt or gets their hopes up, you should know that I took a monster shit on both political parties. If you yourself feel attacked due to your affection for a particular politician or establishment operative, please fight against that. The judging is not of you; it's of the system. A system that paints sell-outs as serious and madness as the mainstream. A system that is proving increasingly dangerous to our political, economic, and social health.

Sooner or later, a campaign like mine was going to happen. I'm sure as hell not the only one who could see that we are politically sick. And I'm not the only one who can see it's going to take a lot more than the red placebo or the blue placebo our current esteemed physicians have been prescribing us.

My mission was never to convert Republican voters into DSA members, fans of the Squad, or disciples of our Lord and Savior Bernie Sanders. My mission was to demystify the Left. To show Republican voters there was nothing to be afraid of in the questions I was asking. To show the nation why the establishment in both parties, as well as the media, were working so hard to portray those questions as a threat.

If only in our district, I feel that mission was a success. Yet this book is not just about me rubbing it in the establishment's face. Nor is it meant to be a political victory lap. It's meant to mark the first lap, in a relay race.

Wouldn't it be something if we could win a dozen seats like mine next go round, maybe a couple dozen? Wouldn't that be a trend worth setting, a history worth making?

I never wanted my candidacy to be seen as the one in a million underdog story it's now celebrated as. I just want it to be seen as something that was possible.

Let's Get Money Out Of Politics And See What Happens

Excerpt from Interview with Jen Brylowski on News 10 WYYB

For the average voter who doesn't follow politics that closely, what do you want them to know about your policy platform?

What I want them to know is that, if you don't have the time to read the detailed and thorough plans on my website, all you've got to understand is that my policies will always be in favor of the most vulnerable to harm and against any interest that benefits from and, because of that benefit, enables such harm.

And to be honest, you don't even have to know what all my policies are. Because if I can get this one thing passed, the others are going to fall into place like they should anyway.

And that one thing is?

Getting money out of politics. If you don't get money out of politics, it doesn't really matter where you stand on any of the issues. Because as long as there is a moneyed interest competing with what the people want, that moneyed interest is either going to win or water down *your* win until it doesn't taste anything like victory. Every issue comes back to this one issue. You fix this, and you go a long way toward fixing the rest.

You know, it's funny. Here we are in primary season, running our campaigns, hundreds of campaigns all across the country. And the truth is, it doesn't really even matter what my stance is on any issue; it doesn't matter what any of these candidates' stances are on any of these issues. If there are donors and lobbyists and revolving doormen telling the majority of your politicians to vote the other way, they're gonna do it.

You're not going to make significant progress, you're not going to find truly just solutions, on any of these issues, as long as there is an industry who has an interest in blocking it and those industries are allowed to fund the political or post-political aspirations of your representatives.

But getting back to policy, do you not concede that your policies are closer to those of the Democrats?

Not until they get money out of politics. Until they get money out of politics, until they try to get money, in a real way, out of politics, I think the Democrats are far greater hypocrites than any of the Republicans.

They're no better because they know better, or they at least claim to know better.

But your policy platform looks nothing like any of the Republicans in the Congress.

You're not getting what I'm saying.

The rest of my policies don't mean a thing if this policy isn't addressed. Until this problem is solved, none of them will get solved. So you can talk about whether someone looks like a Republican or Democrat or whatever label you want to put on them. But until we get money out of politics, I say that we should quit referring to anyone as either Republican or Democrat. Because it's not really honest. You want to be honest, you'll refer to them by the teams they really represent. Look up who their biggest donors are, and that's the team they represent.

Diane Feinstein wasn't Team Democrat; she was Team Real Estate and Team Wall Street. Joe Manchin isn't Team Democrat; he's Team Wall Street and Team Fossil Fuel. Just like Ted Cruz isn't Team Republican; he's Team Real Estate, Team Wall Street and Team Fossil Fuel.

Politicians can caucus under the Republican banner or the Democrat Banner, but if both Mitch McConnell and his Democratic opponent Amy McGrath were funded by Big Pharma, they're Team Big Pharma.

You see what I'm saying? On any given issue, you're not really a Republican or Democrat. You're Team Donor or you're

Team People. And on every issue that comes before me, I want to be Team People.

But for that to matter, we have to get money out of politics. Because any debate we have over any of these policies on the House floor is some phony-ass baloney as long as everyone then leaves the House floor and gets on the phone to fundraise.

What do you say to those, including your primary opponents, who insist that you're just a Democrat?

I would say they're as full of shit *as* the Democrats. And, in fact, for them to say that shows they don't even know what the Democrats are.

It implies that the Democrats really have some kind of ideology. But I don't believe that. I believe the individuals who hold office may have ideologies, but the Party as an institution is not allowed an ideology, unless it complies with the whims of the rich and powerful.

That's why they want you to believe that the only thing that stops a bad guy with a corporate master is a good guy with a corporate master.

I know my policies aren't what Republican voters are used to, but the reason why so many GOP voters have taken a shine to my ass is because I call the Democrats on their shit in a way my opponents can't.

See, my opponents will give you every excuse under the sun why the Democrats vote the way they do. But the truth is if a Democrat gets a call from the same donor base that just gave a call to their Republican counterpart, they're job is to ask how high they can jump and still tell everyone they're better than the Republicans.

And why can't your opponents make that critique?

Because they're ready to jump higher.

So what do you say to Republican voters who don't agree with you on the facts related to key issues?

It's a good question. I run into voters all the time who see the world completely different than I do. And what I always keep in mind is that we may disagree on the surface of the issue, or maybe on every issue. But just below that surface is a place where we most definitely agree. And that is that money has corrupted our politics to the point where they don't know who to trust. It's the reason why Congress has such low approval ratings. It's the reason why populists have done so well in recent showings.

It's no coincidence getting money out of politics has such high numbers, no matter which party you poll. It's because the average voter wants real democracy. But what the average politician tries to feed them is Santa Claus democracy. Where you can put all the shit you want to on your list, but come Christmas morning, your ass, once again, is at the mercy of some old white dude, who has more resources at his fingertips than you can imagine, who doesn't live anywhere near you and who you ain't never gonna meet, but will ultimately be the one making the decision about what does or does not go under your tree.

But your main primary opponent is not an old white man, but rather a woman in her thirties.

I didn't say the politicians were Santa. The politicians are the elves, or maybe a few lucky ones get to be the reindeer. They do what they're told.

Then who's Santa?

Who do you think? The donors are, obviously.

And you think it's that simple?

And you don't?

I'm saying that there are a lot of people who don't see it as being that simple.

And I'm saying that the only way to prove me wrong is to get money out of politics and see what happens. That's all I'm asking.

Let's get money out of politics and see what happens.

Because, see, I have faith that the average voter really does believe their views and their values can win in a fair fight. The problem is we haven't had a fair political fight in decades. Not in the general elections, and not in the primaries.

So let's get money out of politics and see what happens.

If the voters want me out after that, that's fine. If I can help get us to the point where we can see what our democracy actually looks like, my job will be done anyway.

But we've got to get to that point.

Let's get money out of politics and see what happens.

All right, Mr. Valentine, I think we've got it.

Let's get money out of politics and see what happens!

That was H.F. Valentine, running for his district's House seat in the GOP *primary.*

Note:

When I started the campaign, I figured if I had any chance of winning, "Getting Money Out Of Politics" would have to be the cornerstone of my policy platform. No matter what political or economic issue was going to become hot during the run, chances were it could easily be connected back to this one theme. A theme that has wide support by all voters, including even the staunchest of the Republican base.

We'd already seen Republican voters ecstatically cheer on Donald Trump's "Drain The Swamp" rhetoric. And, no, it doesn't matter whether he delivered on the promise. What matters is that the one thing all voters (at least tell themselves they) hate is corruption.

And if you can get Republican voters to focus on corruption as *their* key issue, and you can get them to believe you have a viable solution, or set of solutions, it may be your only chance in overcoming the other ideological obstacles your opponents are going to harp on throughout the campaign.

That's why I used the slogan "Let's get money out of politics and see what happens." While I think you should be strategic in your messaging, it's just as important to be honest. And the truth is if they would have elected a traditional Republican candidate that election and the next election and the next election and so on, shit wasn't going to get better for them. The only way any of us have a chance at seeing what can get significantly better in our lives, and for our country, is if we first get money out of politics.

That's why I told voters that they could vote me out afterwards. Because, at that point, you at least have a real shot at seeing what even traditional candidates might stand for once they are untethered to the pocketbooks of billionaires and multinational corporations. And that is something we have not seen in our lifetimes, and will not see unless we do this one thing.

That's why I'm calling on others to follow my lead. If multiple candidates next time were to pull off these kinds of races by making "Getting Money Out Of Politics" *their* calling card, we might be able to make this issue a priority and turn that momentum into a mandate.

No More Red Placebo No More Blue Placebo

Excerpt from speech for Crossing Party Lines, Barter Hollow Chapter

I got a relative that, back in 2010, called me up and started going on and on about how Barack Obama was a socialist. And I said, "Relative, Barack Obama ain't no socialist." And as you can imagine, he said, "Yes he is a socialist." And I said, "No he's not." And he said, "Yes, he is." And this went back and forth for a little while. And then I asked him, "Relative, do you know any socialists?" And he said, "Hell, nah, I don't know no socialists." Then I said, "Well, how in the hell do you know he's a socialist?" He said, "What do you mean?" I said, "If you really want to know one way or the other whether Barack Obama is a socialist, don't take my word for it. Just go see what all the big shot socialists are saying about him. Find a list of socialist publications in print or online and give 'em a read. See whether they believe Barack Obama is *one of them*." And then we changed the subject, talked about some family shit, and then got off the phone.

Then about two weeks later, phone rung, and it was my relative. I picked up the phone and said, "Hello, relative." He said, "Hey, man. I checked out those socialist publications like you said. Guess what? They can't stand Obama." I said, "Huh, ain't that some shit?" And my relative never referred to Barack Obama as a socialist again. At least not with me.

Now, I tell you that story, not to make fun of my relative, but to illustrate how easy it is for us to be sure about what someone else is or isn't, in spite of us not really having anything to base this declaration on.

And, if we're honest, I think we can admit that we all have done this at one time or another. I know I've done it.

Have you done it? Have you ever caught yourself calling someone a label that you weren't completely sure what the label meant? If I asked five different Republicans right now what a socialist is, I might get twenty different answers. If I asked five different Democrats what a fascist is, I know I'd get twenty different answers. The same goes for words like terrorism or treason or liberal or conservative or right or left or whatever. None of these words are helpful if they're only helpful for the one using it as a weapon.

You know and I know, these labels are, more often than not, just bombs thrown at a political opponent. They don't serve the purpose of understanding, or clarifying, or beginning a good faith discussion. They're just bombs.

And the problem with a bomb like this is that when it's thrown into a political campaign, it doesn't just hurt the candidate it was thrown at. It hurts the voters as well. Because, like I said, it's not meant to ignite healthy debate. It's meant to extinguish it, or prevent it from ever getting started.

And unless we have a clear understanding of who people are and who people are not, outside of the silliness of labels, we're going to continue the destruction of our political process.

So, as a candidate who is Target Numero Uno for such a disingenuous weapon, one of my first tasks is to defuse as many of these bombs as I can before they explode.

The problem is we live in a soundbite world, and you only have so much time to listen to campaign speeches. So as much as I would like to, I can't have a five part debate on what each of these labels is or isn't.

All I can tell you is that I am uninterested in checking off boxes from the Party checklist. Are you interested in that?

I am uninterested in adhering to the demands of a label, letting someone else define me with their particular criteria. Are you interested in that?

I am uninterested in keeping with any political identity constructed by consultants, PR firms, or establishment gurus. I am uninterested in keeping with the wishes of big money campaign donors. Are you interested in that?

My primary opponents are going to say I don't want to address whether I'm this or that. And I'm saying *they* don't want to address the actual work that *they* would do in office. There's a reason why they want to focus on me. And it's so they don't have to focus on themselves. Because they know they have nothing to offer you but the status quo.

And I am uninterested in the status quo.

Are you interested in that?

The truth is, in this game of electoral trickery, these labels can mean pretty much whatever you want them to. In other words, by *their* rules, they don't mean anything.

And if the labels don't really mean anything, then our identities don't have to be what they've told us they have to be. We can be whoever we want to be. We can vote for whoever we want to vote for.

You ever hear one of these Democrats use a negative label to describe their Republican opponent, but when you take a real look at what they're offering policy-wise, it ain't really about shit?

That's them trying to feed you the Blue Placebo. Making you think your cure is in a whole bunch of nothing.

Likewise, when a Republican uses some other label against a Democrat, but ain't really offering anything of substance either, that's them trying to feed you the Red Placebo. Making you think your cure is in a whole bunch of nothing.

Mainstream Democrats and Republicans want you to pay attention to the color of the pill, but not what's inside. Just like my opponents want you to pay attention to an arbitrary label but not what's inside their own campaign. But more than that, they don't want you to pay attention to the policy solutions inside mine.

Every time you hear one of these labels, one of these bombs, thrown at me, remember what I said.

Don't let any candidate, nor anyone in the media, or anyone else attempting to influence you politically, don't let *any* of them fool you with derogatory labels in the service of you believing your cure is in a whole bunch of nothing.

No more Red Placebo.

No more Blue Placebo.

All I'm asking you is to look at what's inside.

Note:

It wasn't hard to foresee that the first and possibly most important problem to solve for a campaign like this would be to diffuse the aforementioned bombs before they exploded, or maybe before they were even thrown. To take these political labels and turn them into boomerangs. Where, if the bastards thought to throw one, they should just assume it's going to come back and blow up in their face. In short, we had to become rubber and make them glue.

We had to make it a shameful act to run a campaign that relies on the intentional ambiguity of labels. We had to convince voters that the very act of using these labels was an affront to their intelligence and their stability. That our opponents were counting on voters being dumb enough to hear a word and then not hear anything else after that. That, if I may use their own tropes, they would be triggered by a mere label and run to the safe space of the status quo.

This didn't mean our opponents were not going to throw these bombs anyway. They most certainly did, and they did because it's pretty much all they had. The test for us was how the media was going to play it. And that meant we were going to have to make the same kinds of criticisms, early on, as it pertained to how the media covered our campaign. The goal being that, whenever the media tried to echo our opponents' smears of this label or that label, we would have done enough work preparing voters for this kind of attack that it would make such media figures look like stooges of the establishment and guardians of the status quo. And, for better or worse, this wasn't that difficult considering the level of distrust Republican voters already had for the majority of corporate media entities.

If done right, the ultimate goal was to benefit from such attacks. To take such rhetorical grenades and transform them midair into political cupcakes. A tasty little gift from our opponents, proving us right about how paper-thin their case really was.

And that's exactly what they turned out to be. Oh so tasty little gifts.

On The Debacle We Loosely Call Healthcare

Beginning of Carter Community College speech

I had someone on the campaign trail ask me the other day, "Mr. Valentine, why are you only harping on the insurance companies? Why not the drug companies too?" And I said, "Because everyone already knows the drug companies are awful. It's such a given nowadays, you hardly even have to make the point."

But after I said it, I thought, "Ain't that some shit? The companies that we rely on to provide us our medicine when we're sick, people just assume they're going to prey on us through advertising, gouge us at the cash register, and lobby against any other beneficial treatments that they either can't control or profit from."

That's the given in America. That's where we're at. That the modern pharmaceutical industry is more akin to weapons manufacturers. Weapons manufacturers aren't interested in peace, they're interested in war. They're not interested in getting to a place where the world needs less weapons; they want to sell more weapons and more weapons and more weapons. And while we are certainly fortunate to have made the advancements we've made in treating illnesses we would otherwise be at the mercy of, the business ethos of our drug makers has advanced far beyond our interests. Between companies less interested in finding cures than they are finding diseases and companies that actively addict us, indeed treating us worse than any street dealer ever would, we're at a place now that we need legislation and the courts to protect us from the companies that make us our medicine. That's where we're at.

And the Congress still hasn't done anything about it. Like they have no power. Or maybe they just don't have any interest.

They sure as hell didn't have any interest when they let a former healthcare lobbyist write key provisions of the Affordable Care Act.

Speaking of, here's how much of a joke our healthcare debate has been over the past two generations.

At the end of the 1980s, the ultra-conservative Heritage Foundation came up with the individual mandate as an alternative to a single payer system. The individual mandate would go on to become part of Romneycare, only to then be borrowed for what would go on to become Obamacare. For which, the Republicans immediately began suing to get rid of the individual mandate.

In the long run, the only thing that any of them could agree on is that we just can't have a single payer system. We just can't have what the rest of the industrialized world has.

And here we are, over ten years after the Affordable Care Act was passed, also known as Obamacare, and the most recent epidemiological study from the Lancet shows that a single payer system like Medicare for All would prevent over 68,000 unnecessary deaths a year, and it would cost less.

Let me repeat that. *Because* we have the system we have right now instead of a single payer system that would cost us less, 68,000 people a year have to die unnecessarily. That's like losing the amount of people we lost on September 11th about every two and a half weeks for an entire year, every year.

And why? Because we just can't have any challenge to our sacred Insurance Companies. Companies that created the crisis we *were* in, when the solution they sold us was the Affordable Care Act. Companies that subsequently carried on their chicanery to the crisis we're in *right now*. Companies that, I might add, provide you and I literally no healthcare. That's right. They don't provide anything. We could streamline the pooling and payment of healthcare dollars, like the rest of the industrialized world does, and the only real difference would be that there's no longer a multi-billion dollar middleman to pick our pockets and deny us coverage. A multi-billion dollar middleman that is seemingly ok with an extra 68,000 deaths a year.

Are you ok with that? Are we ok with that? I know I'm not. Sadly, the most powerful people in our country seem to be ok with that.

Nancy Pelosi is quite possibly the politician most responsible for us not getting a single payer system. Yet Nancy Pelosi knows about the Lancet study. She knows about the 68,000 people a year. But, evidently, she seems to be ok with that.

Mitch McConnell doesn't even want the Affordable Care Act, which at least mandated coverage for pre-existing conditions. Which, if overturned, would mean even more than 68,000 unnecessary deaths a year. But, evidently, he seems to be ok with that.

And it's not just those two; it's the majority of our elected representatives in Washington that seem to be ok with that. And I can say that they're ok with that with quite a bit of confidence because the fix is so easy. It's just doing what every other industrialized nation in the world does, and spending less in the process.

Am I just crazy? The priorities here seem a little out of whack. Maybe I should ask you. What do you think is more important? Saving corporations that literally do not provide healthcare or saving the lives of over 60,000 people and spending less in the process?

Somehow, this is still a debate. Of course, we know the reason why it's still a debate. It's a debate because there's someone else who seems to be ok with that.

I said before that Nancy Pelosi was the most responsible for keeping us from getting a single payer system. But I believe she would not be able to keep us from getting it if it were not for the help of the media. A media who parrots bullshit talking points from the insurance industry and the politicians they bribe.

From NPR to Fox News, whenever Medicare for All is brought up, it's almost like they're obliged to ask how it would be funded. They ask this question as if they don't know the answer. As if they don't know how it's funded in every other industrialized nation in the world that spends a fraction on healthcare while actually covering everyone. They act as if they don't know this.

But here's the thing. They do know this. These aren't yokels who've never been to town before. These are affluent journalists and media professionals who have traveled and seen what it's like all over the world. They know the answer to these questions. And the only reason why they ask them is in the hopes that you don't know the answer. Because here's the other thing. They don't *tell* you the answer. They don't tell you how Canada's system works; they don't tell you how France and Germany's systems work, how it works in Scandinavia or Taiwan. *They* know it, but they don't tell you.

Instead, they leave it an open question. And if they do offer an answer, the answer is always that it will mean raising people's taxes. As if they don't know what premiums are. As if they don't know what copays are. As if they don't know what deductibles are. As if they don't know what out of pocket maximums are. And who knows, maybe they don't know. Maybe they're all so rich, they don't even pay attention to the bills that stress normal people the fuck out. But you know who does know. You know. You know what premiums are, and what copays are, and what deductibles are, and what out of pocket maximums are, and what all these add up to. And what you need to know, the only thing you need to know, is that in a single payer system, you would never have to worry about any of those ever again and you would never have to worry about whether or not you're covered. You would only pay your taxes, and the portion of your taxes going toward healthcare would be less than what you paid before. No more bills. Just automatic coverage.

But they don't tell you that. Corporate media will never volunteer that information. They would rather pretend that it's a debate. As if any of us prefer paying more for getting less.

It's like when they ask people, "Are you ok with Medicare for All if it means losing your current insurance?" And then they go on to talk about this as if anyone in this country actually likes their policy. Are they glad they have coverage? Absolutely. But do they like the millions of miles of fine print they could never wade through to find out if they're going to wind up with a medical bankruptcy even when they have coverage? Hell no. These people act like we love having to worry about going bankrupt, that we love paying more and getting less. They act as if we should be thankful for it.

Otherwise, they would frame the question, "Would you be willing to give up your current health insurance plan if it meant you would be automatically covered with even better insurance - and pay less?" Or how about combining all the facts, and asking, "Would you be ok with far better healthcare coverage if it meant paying less money and ensuring 68,000 extra people don't die this upcoming year?" Or how about asking voters, "Is keeping a worse plan worth the 68,000 unnecessary deaths this system results in each year?"

Ask yourself. Why don't they frame the question like that? It would be completely true; the facts are not even challenged.

That's why I say that they're ok with the deaths. Because you can't even imagine them framing a question like that. They won't volunteer the deaths, they won't volunteer the number of bankruptcies, over half a million a year. They won't volunteer the hassle and the anxiety and the injustice that each and every one of us has experienced as a consequence of the current system.

They won't volunteer it because they're ok with it. And if anyone in the media would like to counter this assertion, there's a simple way for you to prove that you do care. And that's to be honest in the framing of your questions. Quit acting like we don't know our own situations. Quit acting like the deaths don't matter, or the bankruptcies don't matter, like we don't matter. Quit acting like you're just ok with it.

I ask again, are you ok with that?
I'm not.

My opponents like to call me all kinds of names: Democrat, Socialist, Communist, Anarchist, whatever. But what they don't like to call me is an advocate for universal coverage. What they don't like to call me is an advocate to have the best and most efficient healthcare system in the world, because we can. What they don't like to call me is a politician who believes it is immoral and unacceptable in the richest nation in the world for people to have to second guess going to the emergency room because they're afraid it might bankrupt them. What they don't like to call me is a politician who believes it is immoral and unacceptable that even one person should die in the richest nation in the world because they do not have insurance or they have inadequate insurance, much less 68,000 people a year dying for this reason. My opponent will never call me that kind of a person.

I'm advocating for a single payer system, because anything less is immoral and more expensive. Let me say that again. It is immoral. And it is more expensive.

It's bad enough when something is immoral but it is cheaper. That's atrocious on its own. But when something is immoral and costs more, costs much more, what argument is there to keep it? When it is more expensive to be immoral, what argument do you have left?

If Nancy Pelosi won't say it, I will. If Mitch McConnell won't say it, I will. If the corporate media won't say it, I will.

The system we have is immoral, and it is more expensive. It results in 68,000 unnecessary deaths a year, and over half a million medical bankruptcies.

And if my opponents don't like that, they can call me any name they like. Because I don't need to call my opponent names - when I can just call them someone who is ok with that.

Note:

Running in a Republican primary, it's always advantageous to have handy some kind of criticism of top Democrats. And on the issue of healthcare, the criticism was forthcoming.

I don't think it can be stressed enough how disingenuous and dangerous the Democrats' take on healthcare has been over the last decade. Not only did they not learn their lesson, but Barack Obama himself intervened in the 2020 Democratic primary at a time when the candidate running with Medicare for All, a single payer system, as his main policy plank, was ahead in the primary. And he intervened to ensure that that candidate did not win. Barack Obama did that. Now, you can argue it's because he didn't think that Bernie Sanders could win. But that means you believe he thought Joe Biden was a really strong candidate, the same Joe Biden he tried to dissuade from even running.

Barack Obama knew about the Lancet study when he made sure, once again, we didn't get a single payer system. Just like Nancy Pelosi knew about the Lancet study when she, in the same election year, dismissed even the thought that we could have a single payer system. I would contend that the key obstacle in the Congress to Medicare for All was never Mitch McConnell. It was Nancy Pelosi. It was Nancy Pelosi who was sent out to kill even the Public Option in 2009. And here we are, three presidential elections later, talking about the possibility of a half-measure public option being the best we can hope for.

This isn't insignificant. It's everything that is wrong with the Democratic Party. And for any of my critics who think it's unfair for me to pick on Barack Obama or Nancy Pelosi when it comes to the

Herculean task of getting Medicare for All past the Republicans in Congress, I would remind you that they passed the Affordable Care Act using Reconciliation, which bypassed normal Republican opposition. Republican opposition wasn't the issue. Moreover, with the hype of hope and change Barack Obama rode into the White House on, he could have done anything he wanted to in those first two years. Voters were not just ready for serious change; they expected serious change. And now, over a decade later, we still see thousands and thousands of people dying every year unnecessarily.

You don't really believe they thought giving the insurance industry even greater control over our healthcare system was the just thing to do, do you? If so, I offer you the following quote.

"I happen to be a proponent of a single-payer universal health care program. I see no reason why the United States of America, the wealthiest country in the history of the world, spending 14 percent of its gross national product on health care, cannot provide basic health insurance to everybody. And that's what Jim is talking about when he says everybody in, nobody out. A single-payer health care plan, a universal health care plan. That's what I'd like to see. But as all of you know, we may not get there immediately. Because first we've got to take back the White House, we've got to take back the Senate, and we've got to take back the House."

That wasn't Bernie Sanders. That was then State Senator Barack Obama, before he indeed did take back the presidency, the Senate, and the House.

Not satisfied? Then how about these beauties?

"By reasons of security, by reasons of savings. Savings that spring also from the simplicity of the program, savings which spring from early intervention, people seeking and receiving healthcare earlier in the game, so that they don't have more costly healthcare and hospital stays, everything points to Mr. McDermott's bill (the McDermott/Conyers single payer bill). It is interesting to see how under scrutiny, when people really take the look at these bills, how brilliantly the single payer plan stands out... I join my colleagues in requesting from the committee the opportunity for this bill to be considered as a substitute under the rule. It has

support in my community. It has support across the country. It has support in the Congress. I hope it does on this committee as well."

"I remain a staunch and ardent supporter of the McDermott/Conyers bill. One of the principles of the single payer bill is universal access... but for access to be universal it must be affordable... I will join with my colleagues here in working to see that the plan that the Congress passes contains as many of the provisions of single payer as possible, that it does not foreclose on an eventual single payer, and that it does not throw up obstacles to states easily establishing their own single payer."

No, that wasn't Nina Turner. That was the 1990s version of United States Congresswoman Nancy Pelosi.

They *knew* single payer was the only real solution. And whatever happened to them between then and now is a perfect example of why so many Republican voters think the Democrats are full of shit.

The problem is these voters often abhor the arms of hypocrisy while snuggling up in the arms of cruelty. The Republicans tried with every fiber of their political being to repeal Obamacare, with no serious replacement. Meaning the predominant real benefit that made Obamacare worth a shit, that being the coverage for pre-existing conditions, would have been gleefully done away with if the Republicans had their way. Which would have led to even more deaths, far more deaths, than the 68,000 I cited from the Lancet study.

That's why, all throughout my race, I repeated the slogan "I'm not telling you something you don't already know." It's something voters knew. And they knew it because my opponents, by party affiliation, by donor affiliation, had to quite vocally tow the same line against real universal coverage, against even the half measures of Obamacare.

And because it was something everyone already knew, I was able to use that knowledge to illustrate just how much disdain the other candidates had for the voters. How furious these candidates were that their party hadn't been able to scrap what little protections Obamacare had offered and reinstitute a system that once again denied the voters coverage based on pre-existing conditions.

I then did something that far too many lefties can't bring themselves to do. I met Republicans where they are. I appealed to their sense of national pride and told them I didn't want to be just as good as the rest of the industrialized nations. I wanted to be better. If we have the resources to have a superior system, why shouldn't we? Why wouldn't we?

The one advantage we had, the one silver lining in us showing up late to the party, was that we could take the best from all the other countries, and leave behind the things that weren't working, to make a plan that would be the envy of the world.

It doesn't matter if we're last. We can still be Number One. In fact, it's only because we're last that we can ensure we become Number One.

Republicans like talking about being Number One. Why not prove it?

And why not let a Republican lead that charge?

The key to making this a winning issue was not to come out the gate trying to convince a Republican voting base, who've been consistently told by their elected representatives that universal coverage is some kind of communist plot, that a single payer system was the way to go. The key was to meet them where they were. And where they were was being woefully underinsured while shamefully overcharged. Where they were was wanting to have a better system, indeed wanting to be Number One. Where they were was wanting to beat up the Democrats.

So I implored them to ask, "Why do Republicans cede better healthcare to the Democrats?

What if we could finally get real universal coverage and it was a Republican that made the difference, and it was your district that could forever stake claim on that victory?"

I told them if they really wanted to stick it to Nancy Pelosi, then make it a Republican Congressman, your Republican Congressman, the one who would go down in history for doing what she had the power to do but never had the guts to do.

People Hate Politicians

Excerpt from speech given at Tailgate Fest

You want to know the real reason why I'm doing so much better in the polls than was expected? I mean I'd love to believe it's my dashing good looks. I'd love to believe that I've got the perfect policy for every voter. But I know that's not it.

The real reason I'm gaining on these fools is because I'm not a politician. And my opponents are politicians. And people hate politicians. They do. They hate them. They hate their haircuts. They hate their boring suits. They hate the fake folksy just out of the package flannel and denim costume they wear when they're trying to look like the everyman or everywoman. You know what I'm talking about. When they look to make sure the cameras are on them before they roll up their sleeves. People hate that shit.

Just like they hate their stiff-ass body language, and all their rehearsed movements. Like that thing Bill Clinton used to do with that weird broken-ass fist motion, because the consultants told him you can't point into the crowd. And then Obama and Hillary started doing it too. People hate that shit.

And why do they hate it? Because it's fake.

Politicians are fake as armadillo fur.

Just listen to the way they talk. That's what people hate the most. It's the reason why they don't trust them. Because they can see right through them.

Every time I hear a politician on TV refer to "what the American People want," I want to put that politician on a shuttle and shoot them out into space. Because it's soooooo disingenuous. These people don't know what the American People want, because they don't know the American People. They're completely disconnected from what the average person's life is like in America.

When they talk about "what the American People want," they're really just saying whatever their consultants told them you want to hear. Or worse, they're telling you what their donors want. Because as far as they're concerned, that is the American People. Those are the only people that matter.

If they want to better serve us, they could just ask us what we want. And then do it. But they don't. Instead they have to convince us of what it is we want. It's about getting us to think we want what they want, or rather what their donors want.

Case in point. You know what my opponents call no premium, no deductible, no copay, no out of pocket maximum, full coverage, see any doctor you want healthcare? They call it socialized medicine. And they call it that so you'll hate it. So you'll reject it. So you'll continue paying more money and getting worse results.

You know what they call it in all the countries that pay less money and get better results? They call it healthcare.

My opponents, and all their corporate hack mentors, and the industries and billionaires they serve, are fucking lying to you.

They do studies, and polling, and focus groups, and they pour money into consultants and think thanks and economists and every PR hack they can find, all to figure out a delivery that will make things like clear water sound elitist or being able to survive on the planet too expensive.

They don't study us so they can better serve us. They study us so they can better serve us up to their donors. Their big money donors.

Lucky for me, I don't have any big money donors. And I sure as hell don't have any establishment-minded consultants feeding me a bunch of garbage.

Sure, I'm a tad unorthodox. And I may not be as polished or well-rehearsed or even at times as articulate as the other Vampire Robots that pass for Congressional leadership. But when I tell you something, it's because I've listened. I've heard you. It's not because my people did some study or some focus group. It's because I'm taking into account your existence, the life you have to live. Not some fairytale American Dream scenario that sounds good in a campaign speech, but the life *you* have to live. That's what I'm shaping my policies around.

That's why I'm not afraid for you to question my policies. Hell, I want you to question me. I want you to question my policies, because I don't want you walking in that voting booth with doubts.

I admit, when I ask for your vote, I'm selling myself. But I'm not selling my policies. Because I don't have to sell you my policies. Because you don't have to sell someone what they already know.

That's why when I tell you that our current healthcare model is immoral, and more expensive, I'm not telling you something you don't already know.

When I tell white voters that they have more in common with black and brown working people than rich white people, and that if we got together in numbers with our black and brown brothers and sisters, those rich people would no longer be running the show, I'm not telling you something you don't already know.

When I tell Christian voters that being stewards of the earth doesn't mean draining and exploiting our natural resources in a manner that is not only unsustainable for our land, our oceans, and the millions of species that rely on a certain ecosystem to not go extinct, but is antithetical to any semblance of human civilization, I'm not telling you something you don't already know.

When I tell you that our current economic practices have grown inequality and will continue to grow inequality until a literal handful of people will have more money, and thus more political say, than entire countries of people, and that that is unacceptable in any civilized world, I'm not telling you something you don't already know.

When I tell you that we have the money and the resources to be Number One in the world in so many areas, but only if we implement policies that define being Number One in terms of justice and wellbeing for all, I'm not telling you something you don't already know.

When I tell you that it doesn't really matter where any of the candidates stand on any fundamental or structural issues *unless* we can get money out of politics, I'm not telling you something you don't already know.

I'm not telling you something you don't already know; I am merely reminding you of something they want you to forget. Something they will try nonstop with every resource at their disposal to distract you from. To convince you otherwise. To convince you that your eyes are lying eyes.

I'm not telling you something you don't already know. But I am telling you something that my opponents are not allowed to say. And you know why they're not allowed to say it. And you know until we can get money out of politics, they will only ever be able to say what their donors allow them to say. And that means you can never fully trust if what they are saying is benefitting you or benefitting those donors.

What you *can* trust is that I don't owe anyone. Except you. And what I owe you is to be honest and transparent about what I plan to do and why I plan to do it.

Hell, I'm the one encouraging you to question what I'm saying. They're the ones telling you to trust them.

Do you really trust them? Do you really trust the intentions of their big money donors? Do you trust what these legally bribed politicians are telling you?

Or do you trust... what you already know?

Note:

Running as a lefty in a Republican primary, you're already going to be seen as different. You just have to make sure it's a good different.

My team and I had a joke that our campaign was conducting the George Costanza experiment and doing the opposite of what one's political instinct might tell them to do.

Not surprisingly, the media couldn't understand why it was working. Granted, this was the same media that used to make fun of Bernie Sanders' hair, not realizing that was something that voters actually related to. It made Bernie look like a normal person, contrasted with the ambiguously alive, dead, or undead look of Mike Pence.

It was this same establishment presumption of voter superficiality that provided my candidacy its greatest Costanza move. Although we definitely employed our share of slogans and stunts, when it came to my choice of language I resisted the political instinct to simplify. Many even on my own staff, not to mention a number of close friends, had urged me early on to dumb it down. "Don't use too many syllables; don't use too many big words. The speeches can't go on too long." That kind of stuff.

Yet I thought they were selling the voters short. Hell, I knew straight up political simpletons who loved the shit out of Deadwood, and that mess was damn near Shakespearean. Plus, if I heeded their advice, I would only be contributing to the problem.

Propaganda relies on a lazy and unhealthy mind. Our society is sick right now because our political acumen is so weak; our minds are weak. That's how we got to this place. In the early 20th century, workers making a few cents an hour were politically sophisticated. And they demanded more from their society than the crumbs the rich saw fit to give them. That's how this country boomed. Because the workers were too smart to fall for a bunch of bullshit.

What I had to gamble on was that people still had that same capacity in them. Even if they weren't as well-informed. Even if they were being propagandized.

The same way one's eyes and attention gradually correct when switching from screen reading to print reading, it was my suspicion that the longer voters listened to me the more they would get out of it, and that political attention span would prove alive and well. I just had to get them to listen long enough for that to happen.

So in the spirit of transparency, I told voters exactly what I was doing. I told them that I wasn't going to dumb it down like my opponents, like the rest of the establishment political class. I told them I wasn't going to infantilize them; I was going to speak to them like adults, responsible adults.

For certain, I let the slogans do the summarizing. And I repeated those slogans over and over. But behind those slogans was real substance. Substance I believed voters could handle, in language I believed they deserved.

I even gave them reading recommendations on various policy issues, in case they wanted a deeper dive into what I was saying. Did most of them do the reading? Probably not. What mattered was that they could see I was taking them seriously. And that bought me time enough to see if my gamble would pay off.

Quit Letting Them Tell You You're Racist

Excerpt from speech given at Nesbitt Valley Ag Coop

All right, y'all. I'm about to go there.

A lot of people have been waiting to see what a candidate like myself was going to say about race. I've even had people close to me try to steer me away from talking about race. But when I hear that, all I hear is that they believe white people can't be honest with themselves. That Republicans can't be honest with themselves.

And I don't believe that. I believe there's honesty within us, and that if we can just step outside our labels and our political identities, there's so much we can agree on.

Take Black Lives Matter for example.

When someone counters Black Lives Matter with All Lives Matter, they're acting as if they don't understand what Black Lives Matter means. But we know. We know what it means. Because we've seen it before. Just in different words.

We've all seen the iconic pictures from 1968 of black men in Memphis carrying signs that said I Am A Man. We've all seen them.

I want you to think about one of those photos. Think about the men in the picture.

Now I want you to imagine that just outside the frame of that picture there was some white dude with a sign around his neck that said, "I Am A Man Too." I think it's safe to say that damn near everyone in the country today would look at that guy and say he's an asshole.

And yet Black Lives Matter is just this generation's version of I Am A Man. So when you see Black Lives Matter and it just burns you up, you're kind of like the asshole yelling at Dr. King, "Oh yeah? Well, I'm a man too." You're that guy.

The moral of the story being: Don't be that guy. That guy is an asshole. Black people are not asking us for our first born child; they're asking us to recognize the institutional obstacles to equality - and for us not to be assholes.

Or let me try another example.

For white voters who disagree with the sentiment of Black Lives Matter and believe black people are making too big a deal of racism, and that racism isn't really that much of a problem, I would simply remind the women who share this belief just how many men there are still today that dismiss women's stories of sexual harassment, sexual assault, and rape as overblown, claiming that sexism is all in your mind.

I would remind any voters, men or women, who've ever worked a hard job under unsanitary or unsafe conditions, anyone who's had to endure beratement and humiliation from an arrogant or heartless manager, anyone who's had their overtime wages stolen or got screwed out of their benefits and/or a full time shift, anyone who's worked these jobs and are doing the best they can but still find it hard to even stay afloat. I would remind you how many well-off people there are in society who can't see why working people are making such a fuss.

I remind you this not to make you feel guilt, but to illustrate how easy it is for us to dismiss the plight of our neighbors when we do not walk in their shoes.

If you've never had a gun pointed in your face during a traffic stop, it may be hard to imagine it happening to someone else. If you've never been thrown up against a wall and had your body frisked and your pockets emptied when you weren't doing anything but going about your daily business, it may be hard to imagine it happening to someone else. If you've never been beaten or watched a loved one beaten by the very officers who are sworn to protect you and to serve you, it may be hard to imagine that happening to someone else.

But just like the examples above about men not believing women, about the affluent not believing working class people, we have to remind ourselves. Just because it ain't happening to us, don't mean it ain't happening.

And for those who can still see the videos online, can still hear these stories in the news over and over and over and somehow it's still not real for them, somehow they can't understand the justification for the slogan Black Lives Matter, let me try it another way.

Let's do a little thought experiment. When I was a boy growing up, I had a BB gun. And so did the other boys in my neighborhood. In fact, I don't know if I know any men my age who didn't play with either BB guns or toy guns when they were kids.

So when I heard the news about Tamir Rice, I had to try and put myself in that little boy's shoes. I had to think about myself in a park playing with a toy gun, like I had done throughout my own neighborhood. And I had to think about a police car pulling up, and within two seconds of that police car pulling up, I had been shot. And I had to think about how scared I would have been, lying there, knowing I hadn't done anything wrong.

And then I had to put myself in the shoes of that little boy's 14-year-old sister, who saw her brother laying there on the ground and came running to try to help him. And then having the police tackle me to the ground, put handcuffs on me, and throw me in the back of a squad car, like I'm the one who had done something wrong.

And then I had to put myself in the shoes of that little boy's mother and father, processing what had happened, knowing that those cops didn't even administer first aid to my boy as he lay there on the cold ground, bleeding.

But here's the thing. I can try to put myself in their shoes. And I can think about what I would feel if that had happened to me. But the truth is, I can't imagine that happening to me. Because it wouldn't have happened to me.

I remember the first time I heard about Trayvon Martin getting killed. And I thought about if that would have been a white teenager walking home with Skittles and a bottle of tea in his pocket, and it was a black man stalking him in a car, getting out of the car with a gun, and starting a confrontation with him. And when that white child tried his best to defend himself, the black man shot him and killed him. And I thought there is no way in hell that a jury would have let that black man off, nor would the police responding to the scene not arrest that black man. It's unthinkable. And everyone knows it, every white person knows it.

We can't imagine that happening that way. Not in a million years. Just like we can't imagine the police having shot us when we were twelve years old, playing with a BB gun. And it is precisely because we can't imagine that, that more than fifty years after I Am A

Man, black people still have to scream out in the streets of the United States of America that Black Lives Matter.

I can personally name off the top of my head more black people who have been brutalized and/or killed by the people sworn to protect them and to serve them than I can name off the top of my head Presidents of the United States.

This isn't about white people feeling guilt. It's about white people being human, and standing up for others' humanity, standing with our brothers and sisters when they suffer injustice, and until they no longer suffer injustice.

I believe we can do that. I believe we have that in us. That love in us.

Not because it's part of this label or that label or this political identity or that political identity. But from what is inside of us, in what we know is right.

I'm not telling you anything you don't already know. I'm just asking that we listen to our neighbors when they tell us what it's like to walk in their shoes, and that we not be afraid of the questions it will take to get us to a better place.

Note:

There were lots of ways I could have gone about addressing the issue of race and racism. I could have shot holes through the manufactured controversy over critical race theory. I could have done a John Oliver style take down of white supremacist rhetoric throughout right wing media. But that would have been playing on their turf, allowing them to dictate the distractions.

Instead, I chose Black Lives Matter. The driving chant of the biggest protest moment in United States History. Words voters still saw every day on signs and bumper stickers, on shirts and murals. A message that, sadly, many of them still could not digest.

No matter what strategic moves we made with our communication, a campaign like mine needed to stay honest and transparent.

I believed if we were honest, that voters would appreciate it. And as I alluded to in the speech, I think that, outside of their political identity, even the white people who have found themselves hating on or talking shit about or even counter-protesting Black Lives

Matter know deep down that something has to be done in this country to address the inequities that we shamefully still nurture.

The problem is that those who have historically written the Republican newsletter in my constituents' political brain have been telling them to hold their nose so long, a lot of folks have lost their sense of smell. Meaning, the powerful people who run the show don't want walked on and wore out white people to figure out that they have so much more to gain from fighting alongside their black and brown brothers and sisters than they do fighting against them.

And, no, I'm not trying to be conspiratorial. I'm just stating the obvious. It serves the interests of those who benefit from gross inequality to keep those at the bottom, and even those in the middle, of the economic food chain fighting each other over the continuously shrinking leftovers they expect us to call treasure.

Case in Point. You've got to have over 11 and a half million dollars before you even *begin* to pay the estate tax when you kick out. And yet somehow a great number of those who oppose Black Lives Matter also find themselves opposing the Estate Tax. The lesson here being that, to the hardest of hardcore conservatives, Black Lives don't matter nearly as much as rich white deaths.

Now, I tease about that, but the truth is this shit ain't funny. When this country was at its strongest financially, and this is indisputable, the marginal tax rate for the richest folks in the country was over 90 percent and unionization was at its peak.

It ain't no mystery why they want to break the bonds we share. It ain't no mystery why they want to divide working people. The goal is to sow enough animosity amongst us that the status quo becomes a place of refuge for those who are willing to ignore how rough the status quo can get for those with little to no money, power, or advantage.

To dissipate that animosity enough to win this election took more than just one speech. It took a sustained messaging strategy that once again met Republicans where they were. But with an approach far different from my opponents'.

I could have easily pandered to Republicans and told them, "You're not racist." But I don't believe it's that easy. I believe this issue is nuanced and that there's a whole lot more to the story than can be contained within the mere label of racist. What I told

Republicans was that they didn't have to be what they feared that label says to them.

Regardless of whether there is merit to a particular accusation, it is never a fun thing to be told you're a racist. And Republicans especially hate being called racist by Democrats. Yet somehow Republican voters have failed to notice how their own Party leaders and their own ideological figureheads have been jubilantly telling them the same thing.

Sure, we can point out to Republican voters when they as individuals are doing or saying racist things. And, frankly, we should do that.

But I thought it would be far more enlightening, and especially advantageous for this very type of campaign, to point out the ways that their Republican mentors tell them over and over that that's who they really are. That they *are* a bunch of racists.

Because when they tell you that your problem is not those who have the most power in society, those with the connections, those with the direct phone numbers of our law and policy makers, but rather your problem is those with the least power in society, which coincidentally turns out to be black and brown people, they're the ones trying to make you racist, trying to convince you that you're a racist. They're the ones telling you that *that is* who you are.

Not only was my campaign about breaking down the stigma of labels, but it was also to deconstruct what these political identities are and who writes the script. Rather than tell my voters to dismiss racism, I told Republicans they had the power to resist and fight against the pitfalls of white supremacy. But only if they stopped allowing corrupt politicians to feed them lies, to stop allowing those who stand to gain from racial animosity to feed into their insecurities.

In a speech a few weeks later, I proclaimed, "Republicans like my opponents tell you not to let Democrats categorize you as racist, while they're the ones doing everything they can to make you racist. It's like pouring hot fudge over your head and sticking a banana up your ass and then saying how unfair it is that you got put on the dessert menu."

Then I added, "I'm telling you that you have love in your heart, and the conscience and intellect to recognize injustice.

They're telling you you don't have that. Quit letting them tell you that. Quit letting *them* tell you you're racist. Quit letting *them* tell you that's who you are. That your enemy is the masses struggling against racial and economic injustice.

Those masses are not your enemy. They're your neighbors. They're your fellow workers. And they could be your allies in fighting for a better life *for your family*.

Quit letting Republicans, like my opponents, tell you you're racist. Prove to them that you have love in your heart. I know you do.

You have love in your heart. You have love... in your heart."

Comedy Is A Good Bullshit X-Ray

Excerpt from campaign stop at Jack and Jill's (Comedy Club)

Can I be honest with y'all about something? I really try to make sure I'm listening to all my potential voters, and I'm committed to taking everyone seriously. But I don't know about these QAnon folks. I'm kind of scared of them. I'm afraid I'm going to contradict one of them and get imagined into the cabal. I don't want to be a Satan-worshipping cannibal, even if it's just in somebody's imagination.

I got cornered on the campaign trail by a group of QAnon believers. I felt like I was visiting a loved one with Alzheimer's at the nursing home, and the nursing home had gotten taken hostage - by people who spoke a different language. I didn't know what anybody was talking about. All I could do was nod and smile. Lot of nodding and smiling. Don't want to get anybody too upset.

I guess that's the way it is now. It's a brave new world in politics. Now we got Q politicians. I don't know about that. Call me old-fashioned, but I miss a good, solid bribe taker. At least with Mitt Romney we knew what we were getting.

Y'all remember when Mitt Romney said that shit about, "Corporations are people, my friend"? That mofo was sincere, wasn't he? Mitt Romney said, "Corporations are people," like he was sticking up for an oppressed group of human beings. That shit came from the heart.

It was as if one of Mitt Romney's sons had come out *as a corporation* and he wanted everyone to know he wasn't going to love him any less.

"But, Dad, I've always known I was a corporation."

"Well, Son, I had noticed since you were a child you loved to elevate your own interest above others and treat your disregard for the environment as an externality for taxpayers to clean up after the damage has already been done."

Could it be that Mitt Romney is just more accepting than we are? Maybe we're the intolerant ones, and we all misjudged the man. Maybe Mitt Romney was just being an ally.

I will give Mitt Romney one thing though. At least he's a family man. I don't mean personally; I mean politically. In that, you *know* who Mitt Romney's political family is.

The Democrats, on the other hand, are like a deadbeat dad. The moment they need you for something, like the election, all the sudden their absentee asses want to come back around, start spending time with you. Then after the election, they go back home to their other family, their real family, the donors.

And what's worse is that they tell themselves that it was really those big donors that got them all those votes. When the truth is the only thing that big donor money did for their party was make it more fancy. And we all know how awkward it is being at a really fancy party.

Being a proud Democrat nowadays is like bragging that you got into a really fancy party, when in reality you were just that weird naked motherfucker everybody was eating sushi off of. In other words, you're not really *in* the Party. You're just there for show.

Now, I can make jokes about all this, and we can have a little fun with it. But, when it comes down to it, we're laughing not to cry. Because the truth about our political system isn't funny at all.

And the problem is not that it can't be fixed, or that no one wants to fix it. The problem is that we keep looking for solutions where we know we're not going to find them. Because to find the solution, we'd have to admit the problem. Meaning we'd have to actually look in the mirror.

And our politicians don't want to look in the mirror. They don't want to look in the mirror because they don't want to admit that until we get money out of politics, they ain't never going to be able to represent us the way we deserve.

I said until our politicians decide to once and for all get money out of politics, they're just ugly people looking for dirty mirrors. You heard me. Ugly people looking for dirty mirrors.

That's why my opponents can't stand my campaign. That's why the Democratic establishment can't stand my campaign. Because my campaign is about cleaning the mirrors.

Let's clean all the mirrors and see what it is we really look like.

Let's get money out of politics. And see what happens.

Note:

Before I wrote even the first line of the first campaign speech, I went back and watched some old George Carlin stand-up specials. I was reminded that his class analysis was downright radical. I was reminded that his antiwar stance, during the height of the war's popularity, was to the left of Bernie Sanders. And still, Republicans loved, and 'til this day love, some damn George Carlin.

If I was going to get my message across, it was obvious I would need humor. But not just any humor.

People don't remember George Carlin fondly because he was right or left. They remember him fondly because he told the truth.

And making people acknowledge what they know in their hearts to be reality but might otherwise ignore or deny is the kind of truth telling that sometimes only humor can accomplish.

If there is one thing I believe about comedy, it's that the value of good comedy is in demonstrating the importance of self-examination and the virtue of being able to laugh at ourselves. Moreover, I believe comedy is a good bullshit x-ray and that it is better to laugh at the absurd than to let it overtake you.

The question for my campaign was how far we could go, or even should go, and still remain both effective and true to our principles.

If A Tree Falls In The Woods

Excerpt from Interview with Jackie Philbin, 88.7 FM (local NPR affiliate)

Mr. Valentine, you've been very critical of both Democrats and Republicans over the United States' approach to handling Climate Change. What makes your approach better?

Well, I don't know if you can compare our approaches, because I don't think we're trying to solve the same problem.

See, we have a race to cure cancer, not the symptoms of cancer. We have a race to cure Alzheimer's, not the symptoms of Alzheimer's. And yet here we are, in a race to cure Climate Change. Yet Climate Change is not the disease; it's a symptom. And not only is it a symptom, it's the last stage of symptoms.

Maybe just maybe, before our Climate Change solution becomes a death lottery where the bodies are burnt for fuel, we'll realize that we're in a race to cure our minds from the diseased economic logic that puts profits over people, privatizes our commons, and sees our finite resources as an all you can eat buffet.

So are you saying you don't *believe we should be taking measures to reduce greenhouse gases?*

Of course I believe we should be reducing greenhouse gases. I believe we should go so far beyond what our current approach is that it makes the moon shot look like changing your light bulbs. And if you look at my policy proposals regarding Climate Change, you can see that.

What I'm saying is that Climate Change grew out of a set of circumstances. And we have to address those circumstances or else fifty years from now it'll be something else we're trying to figure out how to mitigate and/or adapt to.

All these drug resistant bacteria didn't come out of nowhere. The bees up and dying didn't come out of nowhere. But we keep acting like Climate Change just came out of nowhere.

Denying where all these things come from is still a form of denial. It's a denial that anything but the decay of civilization is going to result from our backwards-ass economic thinking.

It's the reason why all your colleagues in the media debated for years whether there was really a tree falling in the woods.

But the polls show that Climate Change Denial is way down from where it was even a couple years ago.

And that's a good thing. But the problem wasn't just Climate Change Denial. It was the denial of what created it. It's a denial about the greed that rots our economic practices.

It wasn't just the batshit Climate Deniers asking, "If a tree falls in the woods and no one is there to hear it, *are there really woods?*"

It was the rich mofos before them, asking, "If I've got a beaver farm in the middle of the woods, do I have enough money and connections to get the politicians and the media to pretend they don't know why a tree fell?"

So you would, as a Republican Representative, endorse the Green New Deal?

Of course I would endorse it. Hell, I would personally go beyond the Green New Deal. But I also know that we won't get either until we get money out of politics. Until we get money out of politics, we're going to continue on with an economic system that promotes the belief that everything that makes this earth beautiful and habitable must become the sole property of either an individual or a corporation so they can chop it all up into little pieces and sell it back to us like they're doing us some kind of favor.

And what kind of economic system would you propose to replace that?

That's not up to me. That's not for me to design. That's for a truly free and democratic process to develop. The problem is we don't have a democratic process as long as there is money dominating our politics.

I'm not telling you what our economy is going to look like, or even should look like. I'm saying: Let's get money out of politics and see what happens.

Let's get money out of politics and see what happens.

Otherwise, we're just as bad as the Climate Change Deniers.

Note:

For over half a century, we've had enough evidence to acknowledge that fossil fuels are a "can't beat 'em / join 'em" game. Meaning if we can't give up fossil fuels, we're probably going to become fossil fuels. Yet rather than spend hours on the campaign trail going over the mile long detailed list of policy actions I supported, all of which would be far greater than anything being proposed by the current administration, I thought it was more effective to focus on Climate Change as a symptom. And by linking the threat of Climate Change to our focus of getting money out of politics, we were able to show how imperative both tasks are. If we could get money out of politics, it would take out a great deal of the incentive to sabotage our efforts to tackle Climate Change, and would provide even more incentive to go after real solutions.

Plus, it brought Republican voters, some of whom might have still been Climate Change skeptics, back to the central issue of getting money out of politics.

Having said that, I don't believe that we can just gloss over the issue with voters. Soberly describing the threat is important. I believe it is the number one issue/threat the United States and the world faces today, and I personally have no patience for whatever deniers or stallers or obfuscators there are left in the political or media spotlight, nor anyone who still touts an all of the above approach to energy.

If we're going to escape a worst-case Climate scenario, everyone has to understand the responsibility to act. And in a political campaign, that understanding isn't as much a matter of science as it is framing.

When I talked about Climate Change, I talked about the plight of farmers. I talked about access to water. I talked about our children's futures. I constantly referred to the sin of greed. And when highlighting the actual economics of not doing enough, I aligned economic efficiency with the most common comprehension of morality.

But most of all, I revisited the absurdity that is Republican Party authorized political identity.

In a speech I gave toward the end of the primary, I stated, "It's bad enough that the GOP, *and* my primary opponents, have openly surrendered all interest in the issue of better healthcare. Now they tell Republican voters that they must also cede their most *sacred* task to the Democrats, that being Stewardship of the Earth.

Is that what kind of politician you want? Is that what kind of Representative you want? Someone who leaves their work, indeed the most important work that could be done right now, for the Democrats to do?

The question in this election is not whether this is happening. You know it's happening. The question is, Republicans, how long are you going to allow it to happen?"

Blasphemous

Excerpt from Interview with Rachel Barman, KPPX Radio

Mr. Valentine, a large portion of your district is made up of Evangelical Christians. How do you expect to appeal to those voters?

That's kind of a weird question, but ok. I would appeal to them by speaking their language. You know in church sometimes they tell you to stand up and look to the person to your right and say something welcoming to your neighbor and then to turn to your left and do the same thing.

Well, I'm telling my voters to look to the phony politician on this side of me, and then look to the phony politician on that side of me. And then tell those phony politicians, "Phony politicians, you're not my neighbor. Get the fuck out of here. And take your donors with you."

But even that, Mr. Valentine. You must know that cursing like that will turn off a significant portion of Christian voters.

Oh, you think Christians don't curse? You think Christians all sound like June and Ward Cleaver, is that what you're saying? I bet you also don't think Christians drink and smoke weed, or get filthy in the sheets.

Christians live in the world, just like you and me. They're not caricatures. They're people.

Plus, Donald Trump was the President. And curse words were the least of his sins.

But you yourself have said you're an atheist.

What I said was that I'm no longer a believer. And when I say that, what I mean is that I am no longer someone who believes in biblical literalism. Which is not very much different from the bulk of my Christian heroes.

This is really about labels more than anything else. And as I've said over and over, a label can mean anything you want it to mean. That's why my opponents love pointing it out.

But just because I do not subscribe to the label, does not mean I cannot appreciate the teachings of Jesus of Nazareth. In fact, if you are a Christian and you let your faith guide your political participation, I would contend the policies I am advocating for are the closest to the teachings of Jesus of Nazareth of anyone running, and that the policies of my opponents, no matter how Christian they claim to be, are inspired not by those teachings but rather the teachings of Republican Party donors.

Whether it's stewardship of the earth, or how we treat the stranger, or turning the other cheek, or being judged by how we treat the least among us, Jesus' key example was one of being a radical in resistance to injustice.

And if we want to talk about labels, I think that Christians ought to be furious that so many of our politicians, my opponents included, have co-opted the label of Christian for their own political gain and have tried to twist it, to redefine it, as something Jesus of Nazareth would have most certainly railed against.

But your opponents say that it's you *that has co-opted the preacher style of oratory for your campaign. One even went as far as to say it's blasphemous.*

I talk like that because that's the world I was brought up in. So I know that world. I understand that world. And I also understand blasphemy. And what I think is blasphemous is when you use the name of Christ to pimp yourself for corporations.

What I think is blasphemous is turning Christianity into something it's not for political gain.

So I don't really care what my opponents say about me. All I care is what my voters think. And what I would tell my Christian voters is: Don't let them tell you what being a Christian is. Don't let them tell you the Prince of Peace was pro-war. Don't let them tell you the man who flipped over the money changers' tables in the temple would put profit before people. Don't let them tell you the man who washed the feet of the poor would demonize those in poverty and instead do the bidding of billionaires. Don't let them tell you that's who Christ was. That's what's blasphemous. And you know it.

If there's one thing I'm still a biblical literalist on, it's that "it is easier for a camel to go through the eye of a needle than for a rich man to enter the kingdom of God."

My opponents aren't trying to build a better future for the average person. They're trying to build the world's largest needle.

Note:

I'm not gonna lie. This was a big one. Because so many people have consciously or subconsciously tied their political beliefs to their religious beliefs, I cannot understate how easy it would have been to blow it on this one issue.

Running as an unabashed non-believer, it was vital that I took voters' religious identities seriously, something they hadn't really expected a lefty to do. In my district, that meant being knowledgeable of Christianity, to the point of pulling out scripture to counter my opponents' attacks.

Though I was careful not to overdo it. My advantage in the race was that I came to them from a place of honesty, something my opponents could only fake.

As I had bet on, this contrast in honesty provided a persistent element of surprise throughout the campaign, allowing voters who might have otherwise seen me as a godless interloper to instead view my thoughtful but no-bullshit approach as starkly refreshing.

On A Jet, Motherfucker

Excerpt from Sharonwood Amphitheater speech

I'm going to do something today that's normally forbidden in politics. I'm going to talk about the poor.

This is still the richest nation in the world. And in the richest nation in the world, we have a lot of poor people, or people on the verge of being poor.

So what is it that we are expected to believe about this situation?

Because, even when the economy is flailing, both politicians and heralded economists will go out of their way to remind us that we still have the best economic system in the world.

Now, if that's true, that we do have the best economic system in the world, then why's there all these poor people?

Why don't we talk about that?

We talked about sick people every day of the pandemic. The reason we don't talk about poor people in the same way is because we would have to name the sickness.

Because if I'm wrong, and there is no sickness, then the only implication is that poor people deserve to be poor. That if you're poor in America, it's your fault.

But is it really?

Is it the nursing home assistant's fault that the nursing home doesn't pay a living wage even if she works harder and longer hours than the chair of the Holding Company that owns the nursing home? Is it the Walmart worker's fault that Walmart won't give them more hours? Is it the Amazon worker's fault that Amazon will not recognize their human dignity?

Is it the worker's fault that it is so difficult to unionize? Is it then their fault they have no leverage to demand higher wages or better benefits?

Either it's their fault or maybe we don't have as good an economic system as we say we do. Maybe we have an economic system where inequality is the feature and not the bug.

Of course, that's crazy talk. You can't have that conversation. The first notion of that conversation, more specifically the first mention you make of inequality, rich people are going to warn you that what you're talking about sounds a lot like class war.

But, folks, that's kind of what extreme inequality is; it's a class war. Except in their version of class war the only ones who are allowed to say the words "class war" are the ones dropping the bombs.

Imagine that shit. Sitting in a bombed out building and being scolded for crying out over the carnage. Being told you're not the victims; they're the victims. You're the perpetrators, for simply suggesting this level of inequality might be unsustainable.

They say how dare these progressives ask a question like, "Should there be billionaires?" When I say the question doesn't go far enough. What we ought to be asking is, "Should there be rich people? While there are masses and masses of poor people, or people on the verge of being poor, how can we justify having rich people? Do we *really* need for people to be rich?"

And for all those losing their minds over how I could even think up a question like that, I would just remind them that the rich ask the question "Should there be poor people?" all the time. And how do we know this? Because they answer it all the time, and the answer is always "Yes!"

I mean they obviously don't take poverty seriously. These are the same people still repping Trickle Down Economics. That is brazen shit.

"A rising tide lifts all boats!" says the dude who'll never have to worry about the tides - because he's "on a jet, motherfucker - on a jet, motherfucker. In the air, motherfucker, you like ants, motherfuckers."

Now, the funny thing is, when the stories run about what I said here today, the thing they'll focus on is that I said motherfucker. They won't focus on the fact that mainstream economic thought is the gaslighting of the century.

They won't mention that, since the 80s, they've been implying that poor people have only themselves to blame. Which is like asking some poor slob that just got his job outsourced what he was wearing before he got the news. That's the game. Victim blaming and poor shaming. Tout meritocracy and deny privilege. Never mind that poor shaming those with the least advantages is like calling your ten-year-old kid a piece of shit because he can't throw the football as far as Tom Brady.

They want you to believe that if you're poor in the land of milk and honey, it's either a moral failing or something to do with your "culture." Of course, we all know what "culture" is code for. And whether it's the "culture" of poor black and brown people or the moral failings of "poor white trash," the point is to make you believe: There ain't nothing wrong with the economy; there's something wrong with you.

The problem is that it's not just the poor anymore who are falling victim to the feature of extreme inequality. As inequality accelerates, the middle class is seeing more and more casualties of their own.

And the only way they can distract us from the class war being waged on us is to turn our soldiers against each other.

Now, that may sound absurd. That an army could not even know when they're in a war, and some segment of that army could actually be fooled into taking orders from the enemy. Sadly, that's exactly what's happened. And the only way something so absurd can be accomplished is if people don't know who their fellow soldiers are, and they forget how wars actually work.

Because this war is not unlike other wars, in that the shots are called by those at the top, and poor and working class people are expected to do the bulk of the fighting. It's just that in a Class War, we're expected to fight each other, and not the side perpetrating the war.

But you know what? I'm not telling you something you don't really already know. I'm just asking you to look around, and get reacquainted with your fellow soldiers.

I'm asking you to realize the power we possess when we fight together.

We have the power. Not just to fight this war, but to end it.

Note:

While most politicians are loath to talk in any serious way about people being poor, I jumped right in.

We all know no one wants to be poor. Why avoid the issue? I kept a policy focus on growing and extreme inequality because so often fear works. And, in this case, the fear is warranted.

Many in what we call the working class could be considered poor or on the verge of being poor. Furthermore, when you factor in debt and the precarious nature of employment among many who would be considered semi-affluent, it's not hard to see how many potential poor people the middle class has waiting to be economically birthed.

My opponents couldn't talk candidly about inequality because my opponents still wanted voters to believe our economic system is solid. But here's how you know it's not.

You know the economy is in trouble when politicians are finally talking about "the working class." And the only reason why politicians found themselves talking about the working class is because so many in the middle class got poorer.

Eventually, they'll get around to using the term "the working poor."

That's when you'll know it's too late for political debate.

The FTS Caucus

Excerpt from Interview with Jeff Hall, Channel-8 WFMU

What do you say to voters who say that H.F. Valentine isn't one of us?

I'd tell them to think about what they mean by "one of us." Because I ain't one of these carpetbagging candidates like Hillary Clinton, who moved to New York and told everyone she deserved a Senate seat. Hell, I'm from the district where I'm running.

I'd tell them, "I have the same social and cultural references that you all have. And I'm closer to you than any multi-millionaire politician wined and dined by Washington lobbyists ever was and ever will be."

I'd tell them, "You think these old school Republicans in Congress know what your daily existence looks like? If they did, their biggest fight in the last ten years would have been something in your interest, and not tax cuts for the rich."

But that's just it. Some hear you denounce Republican tax policy and say you can't possibly be a Republican.

That's because we think in terms of rigid political labels.

Then what label would you prefer?

None of them. Because none of them really mean anything, if they can be twisted to mean anything. If you need to identify me by some concrete political vision, I would prefer to be known as the dude who wants better education for his kids, just like you. The dude who wants better healthcare for his family and neighbors, just like you. The dude who wants strong roads and bridges so my car don't fall into a giant hole in the highway like some b-rate horror movie.

I want air that doesn't make me question if it's a good idea to go for a walk and water that doesn't make me think about holding it up to the light before drinking it. I want an agricultural system that doesn't kill bees or family farms, and I want a planet I don't have to fear for. Dare I say, just like you.

I'm uninterested in what you choose to call me, just like I'm uninterested in what rival campaigns choose to call me. You could put all the bad labels together for all I care. Call me a Commulist Anarcrat. No consultant-manufactured descriptor is going to change the fact that I want the same things in my life as the voters want in theirs.

But you can't deny, if you were to win, your policies would be closer to those of the Squad than Republican leadership in the House.

And you can't deny the only reason why the Squad is in the Democratic Party is because we don't have a parliamentary system.

You think the Squad enjoys being in a party with Nancy Pelosi? Hell no.

They live in blue districts, and I live in a district that is Ronnie Reagan Red.

So you're essentially saying you would be a Democrat if you lived in a blue district.

If I lived in a blue district, I would be just what I am right now. An independent playing the game, a game I did not write the rules to, but one I intend on winning. Not for me, but for all of us.

I'm not running to make a statement. I'm running to win. And in my district that means running as a Republican. But more than that, it means asking Republican voters to take a long look at what it means to *be* a Republican. As well as asking why they agree with the majority of my policy positions, but everybody in the pundit world is screaming at them that I couldn't possibly be "one of them."

Why not run third party?

Why would I? If I wanted to run third party and lose, I'd run for President.

Third party. You act like we live in the future. I'd have a better chance of becoming Mayor of Mars.

Seriously, why run third party and lose, when you can interparty caucus and get shit done?

What do you mean by interparty caucus?

Just what I said. When I get to Congress, I'm looking to get shit done. I'm not here to be a nobody in my party. I'm here to be a somebody in a caucus.

But there are no interparty caucuses.

Well, there will be come Election Day. See, I know why you're asking all this. You're trying to be polite. But just go ahead and say it. Am I going to be a Trojan Horse? Am I going to get through the gates and then unleash common-sense, uncorrupted policies to improve the quality of life of the average citizen? Yes I am. I am going to be that Trojan Horse.

I don't know if your candidacy is being described as a Trojan Horse as much as it is a Manchurian Candidacy.

Oh, I'm not a Manchurian Candidate. I'm something far more dangerous than that. I'm an honest man with a crooked plan.

See, I don't need a third party, when I can just start my own caucus. A caucus open to Republicans and Democrats, but closed to lobbyists and big business.

But why a caucus?

Because there's power in numbers. If you're one outlier in a party, even if you're saying what voters have been waiting to hear, they, being the Party and the media, can paint you as a loon and ignore you. But if you're part of a *group* of outliers saying the things that voters have waited their whole lives to hear a politician say? Well, then they gotta take your ass seriously.

And what do you plan to call this caucus?

I'm calling it the FTS Caucus.

And what does FTS stand for?

It stands for the reaction that each and every one of us feel when we're faced with the reality of where we're at in America. To put it plainly, it stands for "Fuck That Shit." As in, inequality is at the highest levels since the Great Depression? Fuck that shit! We spent a trillion dollars on a military plane that we ain't never gonna use? Fuck that shit! Countries all over the world subsidize college, and we got elementary teachers paying for school supplies out of their own money? FUCK THAT SHIT!

And if you don't like the F-word, then we can skip to the co-meaning of the FTS Caucus. And that is to "Fix That Shit." Because, see, this isn't just about complaining; this is about finding solutions. Health insurance premiums are still too high with crazy-ass deductibles, and I still could go bankrupt? Well, if we institute a universal coverage single payer system like the rest of the world has, we just fixed that shit.

And you're serious about this?

Hell, yeah, I'm serious. If you've got an interparty caucus, you don't need a third party. If you've got flex membership, you can tackle all kinds of issues.

What does that mean, flex membership?

It means membership in the FTS caucus is on an issue by issue basis. Meaning someone can join with the FTS caucus on a specific issue, and once that shit is fixed, they can go back and tow whatever party line they want.

Because, remember, hardly any of these solutions are supported by the establishment in either party. So it's not like you're going over to the other side. You're just acknowledging that no party is perfect and some issues can't wait on the Hatfields and the McCoys to go bowling together.

But who makes the policies?

The permanent members of the caucus. And that doesn't mean permanent members have to vote with the caucus on every issue either. There may be an issue here or there where they disagree with the other members. And that's ok. As long as they stand with us on the issues we agree on, then we maintain our impact. So between permanent members and those willing to temporarily join us on issues that simply can't wait forever, we should at least start moving toward getting some shit done.

But what about the language? You've been criticized before about your language, and the name of the caucus you're proposing uses profanity for two of the three words in its name.

What do you want me to say? If you don't want to say fuck that shit, say forget that shit, and then say fix that shit. If you don't want to say shit, then say stuff. Or better yet say system. We have to fix our system, because right now our system is broke as... well, I think you know what I want to say.

Look, I know some people are sensitive about so-called profanity. But are they more turned off by a string of letters than they are someone serving a 10-year sentence for stealing a sandwich? Are they more turned off by a dirty word than they are the fact that half a million people are homeless in the richest nation in the world?

I was referring more to parents who might not want their children to hear such words used by a political leader in Washington.

Then don't let your kids watch my campaign video. You know what - on second thought, let your kids watch my campaign video. Because this is the shit they're gonna have to be dealing with if you don't elect fools like me to shoot straight with your ass.

So yeah, kids, excuse my language but don't excuse these assholes in Congress. Tell your parents to quit bullshitting with your future and vote for candidates who pledge to be in the FTS Caucus. It's the least they can do, if they're not assholes too.

Note:

There was no getting around having to defend, which is why we *preemptively* defended, against the grumblings of such a candidacy being a Trojan Horse or some Manchurian bullshit.

It's why, during the campaign, I talked openly about *what I mean* when I say the word "radical." Because so much of the media, and so many politicians, like to define the term the same way they define extremism, I figured a lot of not-so-political folks and middle-of-the-road voters might hear the word radical thrown around, and it would be scary to them.

But, as I said on the campaign trail, the word radical, in the sense that I use it and the people who share my beliefs use it, simply derives from the Latin "radic" or "radix," meaning "root." So when I say that I'm radical in my politics, it just means that I believe to get to a solution, you have to look at the root of the problem. That's why I talk so much about money in politics. I believe the legalized bribery institutionalized into our political system is the root of so many of our policy problems.

In a speech I gave later that week, I said, "So when you hear me use words like radical or revolutionary or institutional or structural, it just means that I'm looking to the actual roots of the issue in how to address it. Furthermore, I see no reason to hide the fact that not only am I radical in my political views, I am radical in my economic views. I personally advocate for moving beyond capitalism to a better system. And for any of those listening who are saying, 'I knew it. I knew it. I knew this campaign wasn't about politics, but really about brainwashing me into being one of those Pinko Commie Bastards my uncle used to talk about,' I'm sorry to disappoint you. That's not what this campaign is about. I personally want to move beyond market and centrally planned socialism as well. The reason why I'm bringing all this up is the same reason why I think it's important for a lefty candidate running in a GOP primary to be transparent about their motives. All this campaign is really about is freeing up our political system from the grip of corruption and seeing where democracy actually takes us. And that's all getting money out of politics is about. Seeing where democracy actually takes us."

After that speech, pundits were placing bets on when I would leave the race. They just couldn't imagine a Republican primary candidate explicitly saying they wanted out of capitalism and still being considered viable. But I knew that if you can get people to take you seriously, based upon nothing more than their belief that you are an honest person, they will listen to what you have to say. They may not follow you into the revolution, but they will give you the benefit of the doubt. And that's really all you can ask for.

Take This Job

Campaign Ad

You believe in hard work. And you work hard. So when you see some guy next to you not working hard and making the same money as you, it burns you up. Well, what about someone not working as hard as you making two times what you make? Or what about someone making ten times, or a hundred times? What about someone making 300 times what you make and not even coming close to working as hard as you?

It's easy to focus our anger on the guy next to us. But did you ever stop to think that maybe that guy's not working as hard because he also sees the CEO making all that money, and he thinks that's some bullshit. Maybe that guy ain't about being no chump.

Maybe you and that guy need to get together and start organizing others. Form a union. Demand higher wages and better benefits. Demand half the seats on the board. And if the chance ever arises to pool your resources together and buy that company or to start your own worker-run cooperative, you show 'em - that you don't need some fancy CEO making 300 hundred times what you make. You just need each other.

Oh, and there's one more thing you need. Someone in the Congress who'll fight like hell to make those things a lot easier to accomplish. Someone in Congress who also knows this is some bullshit, but doesn't have that fancy CEO and their fancy friends padding his campaign coffers. Someone in Congress who ain't about being no chump.

My name is H.F. Valentine, and *you know* I approve this message.

Note:

While I ended the ad focusing on solutions rather than just the problem, I don't want to lose sight that, in America, there has been a lack of adequate anger toward, or even notice of, the assholes at the top making literally 300 times what the average worker in that respective company makes. That's some real statistics. That shit is happening.

Instead, working people in this country have been so disempowered that often they feel lucky to even have a job.

I remember, when I was a kid, one of the first songs I ever learned to sing was a Johnny Paycheck song where Johnny Paycheck said, "Take this job and shove it, I ain't working here no more." And you know what? It was a hit. They played that song on the radio. Everybody was singing it. A couple years after that, "9 to 5" came out. It became another smash hit. Everybody was singing that.

Fast forward forty years and now instead of singing "take this job and shove it" they've got fools singing "take this job and love it." Not to mention, "9 to 5" got repurposed for a goddamn gig economy Super Bowl ad genuinely encouraging people to work more than the hard won 40 hour work week.

Moreover, after four decades of telling people what's good for the owners is good for the workers, only then to tell workers if they want to get ahead they'd better get a side hustle or two, far too many of us have traded in hope for raw cynicism.

When fast food workers started the Fight for Fifteen, I heard other working people actually mocking those calls. Instead of supporting their fellow workers, many were suspicious of them. They found themselves comparing the work they did and how they did it to the drive-thru worker in their mind, rather than comparing their everyday effort and sacrifice to that of someone like Jeff Bezos.

And when you're already in that mindset, is it really a surprise that voters find themselves choosing candidates who end up doing everything they can to keep wages low and unions nonexistent?

I railed on this in my campaign not to shame voters or make fun of them, but to at least get my voters asking, "What the fuck *is* going on? Why are we putting up with so much foul shit at work? Why are we making the bosses arguments for them? Why are we glorifying bosses in the first place? Why is more and more work the only answer? And most importantly, why are unions and collective bargaining power absent from the political identity of Republicans?"

When it comes to the rich and powerful in this country, all we've got is our numbers and their benevolence. And their benevolence ain't been about shit. I think it's time we start looking at what we can actually do with our numbers.

Hitting My Quota

Excerpt from Interview on the Kiss Me I'm Conservative podcast

Mr. Valentine, last week you were making a point about the danger of romanticizing the past, and you compared former President George W. Bush to a car with no seat belts.

No, get it right. I said that Democrats during the Trump administration helping resurrect the reputation of George W. were like older car enthusiasts being nostalgic about how awesome the Chevrolet Corvaire looked compared to the ugly shit we're driving around in today. Forgetting that the Corvaire didn't have any seatbelts and was deemed unsafe at any speed.

But that gets to my point. Don't you worry that kind of criticism of two former Republican presidents will hurt you with the voters?

Wait, did I not hit my quota that day?

What quota? What are you saying?

My quota of badmouthing Democrats. Isn't that how the game works? Once I make a certain amount of fun of Democrats, then I'm ok to make a little bit of fun of Republicans?

It sounds like you're joking, but I can't really tell.

That's because I kinda am and I'm kinda not. See, when I first assembled my campaign team, one of my team members told me that when it came to my criticism of Republican policies and policymakers, I had to give to get. Meaning if I was going to shit on Mitch McConnell, I had to first shit on Nancy Pelosi. Which was fine with me, because both deserve it.

So are you saying you're being disingenuous when you critique Nancy Pelosi?

No, see, you're hearing what you want your listeners to hear, what you think will get you more shares. What I said is that they both deserve it. The truth of the matter is that running in a Republican primary is actually quite liberating. Because it allows me to say things, *on* the campaign trail and once I win, that I wouldn't be able to say if I were running as a Democrat.

Like what?

Like how Nancy Pelosi is on the record admitting the reason for her power is because she's the biggest fundraiser for the Party. And that's what in some ways makes her even more corrupt than Mitch McConnell. Because she knows better.

What do you mean by that?

Well, just take healthcare for example. In the 90s, Nancy Pelosi was asking the Congress to take up a vote on a single payer system. Now she's the main obstruction for Single Payer.

That's not because she spent the last twenty five years on the phone with voters. It's because she spent the last twenty five years on the phone with donors.

Think about that. Look at what the system has done to this person. In another world, she might not have turned out that way.

That's why I want to get money out of politics. To save the Nancy Pelosis of the future.

If liberals want to ignore what's happened to their party's political leadership, that's on them. But none of us should ignore what this system is doing to us.

And what is it you think it's doing to us?

It's distracting us. It's distorting our values and redefining our priorities. It's deteriorating our critical thinking skills. It's making us hypocrites.

Does that go for the more progressive Democrats as well?

Depends on the issue. I know the Republican leadership thinks the Squad makes for a good villain. But I personally think Republican voters ought to respect the hell out of a Rashida Tlaib and an Ilhan Omar, or a Cori Bush and a Jamaal Bowman. They're smart, they're competent, and they're at least trying to represent what their voters actually want. You may not like what their voters want, but that's ok. You don't live in their district. And no matter how much it may burn your eyes to look at the faces that get taped onto Republican dartboards, whether it's over policy or their style of delivery, or even their strategy, none of which is always going to be the right one, one thing you have to give them is they're not bought. And there's very few voters in the United States who can say that about their own representatives in DC.

And I'm serious when I say that. Republicans ought to love progressive Democrats. Because the biggest bee in Nancy Pelosi's bonnet isn't Kevin McCarthy. It's the threat that one day there's going to be enough unbought Democrats elected that her exit and legacy will be one of utter and lasting shame.

Now, the advantage I have over the Squad or the Squad 2.0 is that I can tell the Democratic leadership what the Squad would love to tell them but can't. And because of the nature and brand of my unprecedented campaign, I can also tell the Republican leadership what I think of them. And I pledge to do that again and again once I'm elected.

That's why I'm so much higher in the polls than y'all predicted in the beginning of this thing. Because the average person can't stand the average politician. And if they can elect a person to go to Washington that they know will find the phonies in either party and will tell them about themselves to their phony faces on the floor of the Congress? Well, to a lot of people, that's worth a vote by itself.

Note:

How do you talk about Democrats and Republicans in a campaign like this? What can you get away with saying and still have a shot at winning? Is there a line? Or is crossing the line the whole point?

My team and I felt it was safe to assume that you can talk relatively funky about Democrats in any Republican primary in the nation. But we also suspected that you could talk a lot funkier about Republicans than would normally be advised, as long as the criticism was aimed at corruption in Congress.

The bigger question was, if we actually won, would this strategy come back to haunt us? It's one thing to get elected. It's another to get shit passed and be an effective legislator.

Our answer was to keep calling the bastards out, but to keep our aim high and, unless provoked into a fight, primarily target those toward the top. Which may sound counterintuitive at first (considering who doles out the committee appointments), until you acknowledge that Party leadership's long grip on power is precisely due to them not getting publicly challenged and there not being a sustained challenge to the Party narrative. It may not be an overnight-results strategy, but it's the only way to get the media paying and bringing attention to the disparity between policy and people's lives.

Plus, people like fighters. And they especially like underdogs. If I can help a few more of my ilk get elected, we may be able to change the narrative enough to make it easier for others to get in the fight as well.

Until we fully get money out of politics, it's all a fucking game. Members of Congress are nothing if not ambitious. And, phony or not, they love to pretend like they're fighters too. The point is not whether they believe in what they're fighting for; it's what impact the policy will have on the people.

I wish it wasn't that cynical, but it is. I also wish fighting for a demonstrably better future didn't come with trolls, betrayals, and death threats. But it does. At least for now.

At least for now, this is the task ahead. And like the old saying goes, "It's a dirty job... so somebody's gotta kick the boss's ass and demand cleaner working conditions."

End of Humphries Memorial COGIC speech

I'd like to read you a few words from Republican President Dwight D. Eisenhower's farewell speech.

He said, "Disarmament, with mutual honor and confidence, is a continuing imperative. Together we must learn how to compose differences, not with arms, but with intellect and decent purpose.

I wish I could say tonight that a lasting peace is in sight."

He said those words after he said these words.

"In the councils of government, we must guard against the acquisition of unwarranted influence, whether sought or unsought, by the military industrial congressional complex. The potential for the disastrous rise of misplaced power exists and will persist.

We must never let the weight of this combination endanger our liberties or democratic processes. We should take nothing for granted. Only an alert and knowledgeable citizenry can compel the proper meshing of the huge industrial and military machinery of defense with our peaceful methods and goals, so that security and liberty may prosper together."

Did you get that? Only an alert and knowledgeable citizenry. We should take nothing for granted.

Now, some who've heard this before will recognize that, in the actual speech, President Eisenhower only said "military industrial complex," and that I added the Congressional part. But actually the original speech said just that: Military Industrial Congressional Complex. And they took the Congressional part out because they wanted to make it more palatable to the Congress. And yet 60 years later, I think we can see that playing nice with the Congress has not worked. I said 60 years, trillions and trillions of tax dollars that cannot be properly accounted for, and dozens of countries unconstitutionally attacked later, any objective review of the Congress's role in managing our "defense" efforts would be hard-pressed to limit the number of times it used the word obscenity in its summarization.

Once military spending became a measure of business and then consequently jobs, the reckless application of our war resources was inevitable, until eventually our war officials became more economists of violence than keepers of peace.

The same way business economists came up with the term "externalities" to describe things like industrial-polluted water, land, and air, our economists of violence began using words like "collateral damage" to describe families blown to pieces by US tax dollar funded missiles.

And for anyone who would even suggest that I am misrepresenting even one year of this history of U.S. foreign policy, I would challenge you to find even one instance of that policy in which we would have found acceptable the same posture taken towards us that we took towards our adversary.

All of this is to say the key guiding principle in my foreign policy will be something all my voters can understand and are familiar with. And that is the Golden Rule.

We cannot claim to be a moral nation if we cannot apply even the most basic of moral principles to our conduct on the world stage.

Neither can we claim to be a moral nation if our budget sacrifices the basic necessities of its citizenry in the name of defense expenditures so unconcerned with our actual defense that they don't take into account the two massive oceans separating us from any enemy, imagined or real.

This does not mean we should not prepare for the worst. It means that we can't let such preparation become a self-fulfilling prophecy. And we must no longer let the business model of the Military Industrial Congressional Complex supersede our responsibility to treat others as we would have them treat us.

To be safe, to be secure, it requires that we be an alert and knowledgeable citizenry. And that we should take nothing for granted. To be a moral nation adhering to our most basic moral principle, it also requires that we be an alert and knowledgeable citizenry. And that we should take nothing for granted.

Note:

Although it may not poll as a top dinner table issue, foreign policy is still an aircraft carrier sized discussion. As Noam Chomsky rightly explains, outside of Climate Change, nuclear annihilation is humanity's greatest threat. And our nuclear posture on the world stage is only a fragment of the complex web that weaves our relations with other nations.

Within this web, there are so many angles and consequences that the task may seem daunting to even grasp. And yet, I do believe we can apply a couple basic guiding principles to our foreign policy vision that would keep us within the framework of being a just nation.

The first being, throw all that intention shit out the window. It don't mean dick. The rule has to be Anticipated Consequences. If you do a drive-by on the dude's house that beat your ass in front of your girlfriend and your mama last week, you can't go to court talking about your intention was just to test out the latest Uzi model. (Ok, maybe that's not the best example. But you get the picture.) You can always say your intention was something other than the actual horrific consequences of your actions. The question is not what your intentions were. The question is what were the anticipated consequences. And whether it's foreign policy or in everyday domestic life, we have to think in terms of and must expect to be judged by what anticipated consequences our actions will bring.

Secondly, we have to be ready to apply the same principles to ourselves as we apply to other nations. If one of our adversaries started erecting military bases and storing missiles off our coast, we would shit Tabasco Sauce. And yet we think it's completely ok if our Army Base map looks like we shot the globe with Military Industrial buckshot.

On a side note, however less eloquent my translation may be, these two principles come courtesy once again from your friend and mine Noam Chomsky. Noam's contribution just can't be overstated. If you haven't already done so, do yourself a favor and check him out. Most of the people I admire attribute a large chunk of their political education to his work. And I damn sure wouldn't be where I'm at today if I hadn't found his writing.

Don't Hate The Player. Call Out The Game.

Excerpt from first Interview with Greg Killebrew, MSNBC

Mr. Valentine, it's not a stretch to say that you are the least popular candidate.

Popular? Popular with who? Because I know you're not talking about the voters. The only reason why you're interviewing me right now is because of ratings. Which means that the people can't get enough of what I'm saying.

Now, if you're saying I'm not popular with the colleagues I'm going to serve with, you're absolutely right. Which is one of the reasons why the voters can't get enough of what I'm saying. I know the Congress can't stand me. But you know what, people can't stand the Congress. And I don't mind being the middle finger they send to the Congress. I don't mind it because the Congress deserves it.

Seriously, these politicians and think tanks and, yes, journalists are not mad because I'm brash, or because I curse too much, or because I don't have the right haircut. They're mad about the clarity with which I'm shining a light onto corruption within our political system, and the institutions that facilitate such corruption.

So give us an example of what you're talking about when you say corruption?

Are you kidding me? Are you kidding me with that question? You think that's journalism? Asking for evidence of corruption in DC? Asking for evidence of corruption in DC is like asking for evidence of photosynthesis while standing in a garden. The better question would be, "Can you name me one issue where there isn't some kind of moneyed interest working behind the scenes to control both the vote and the media narrative?"

Why do you always seem so hostile toward the media?

Because y'all are fucking us. Every time y'all act like you can't tell whether the sky is really blue or not...

Mr. Valentine, we're not going to allow you to be abusive. If you can't be civil in your language, we're going to end the interview.

Oh, what, you mean the cursing? You don't want me to curse? Ok, I won't curse. But don't give me any of that stuff about being civil. Because I think we got different definitions of what it means to be civil. And I think your definition of being civil is not upsetting your advertisers or the establishment powerbrokers you want to keep access to.

I know you like to think you're above the fray. But y'all ain't no better than the politicians. Y'all put y'all's interest before the interest of your audience every day of the week.

And just how do we do that?

By picking the lowest hanging fruit for yourselves and then acting like the rest of the fruit is out of reach.

I don't even know what that's supposed to mean.

It means y'all patted y'allself on the back for calling Donald Trump's claims about the election a lie. But you spent two decades saying he-said/she-said about Climate Change. Y'all patted y'allself on the back for debunking anti-vaxxer claims. But you've spent a decade acting like you don't know the facts on single payer healthcare.

If I'm not mistaken, y'all haven't even properly apologized for the way you covered the lead up to the War in Iraq. That's a million dead on your head. And you want to talk about curse words?

I'm not here to re-litigate the Iraq War. I'm here to...

Then what are you here for? Because it sure ain't fact checking my policy claims. The only thing y'all ever do is act like my campaign isn't serious or try to call me out for something I said the wrong way.

But you know what? You ain't calling me out. I'm calling you out.

You're the ones who have to answer. Not me. I'm for ending the preventable deaths of over 60,000 people a year and saving money while doing it, like every other industrialized nation on the planet. You're the ones who have to answer for why you've pretended this not to be the case.

I'm the one for doing whatever it takes to save our species from Climate Change. You're the ones who perpetuated Denialism with he-said/she-said *and* brought on economists to tell us saving our way of life was too expensive. You're the ones who did that. Not me. You have to answer for that.

I think you're mischaracterizing our reporting.

Oh, is that what you think? Then prove me wrong. Because, you know what? I'll give you a break. How about you don't have to answer for any of what I just said if you commit right here right now to quit bullshitting the American public.

Quit confining your reporting to conventional wisdom; quit having on pundits to your shows who don't ever have to suffer the consequences of the topic you're talking about. Quit doing softball interviews with people who have proven to be just fine with the status quo. Quit all of that and start giving the people a little humanity.

And if you can't quit all that, then you're the ones who are going to have to answer. Not to me, but to the viewers and readers who smell the status quo stink all over you.

I think this interview is over.

It's only over because you know I'm right.

No, I don't think you're right. I think you're being unfair.

Well, like I said, if you think I'm being unfair, then prove me wrong.

Start proving me wrong. Do better. Tell the truth and not just what each side says, like there's no context, like there's no other side. There's more than the frame they allow you.

Take a walk around outside the status quo. You might just like it.

I can assure you that no one tells us what to say.

Ain't nobody got to tell you what to say. You just got to know what you'll be rewarded for saying. And what you'll be not rewarded for saying. I mean I shouldn't have to tell you to read Manufacturing Consent. You should care enough about journalism to have already read it.

But you should read it. You should try stepping outside of that framework they expect you to think in. There's a whole world out here.

You should join me in it. It's freeing. It really is.

Thank you for your time, Mr. Valentine.

I'm serious now. I'll be right here.

When you're ready, I'll take you on the tour.

Goodbye, Mr. Valentine.

Note:

Even more important than calling out the hypocrisy of our primary opponents, my team and I made it our mission to whip the corporate think out of each and every journalist we encountered.

Now, some might think that's a dangerous strategy considering we were going to have to rely on news coverage if we had any possibility of winning. The problem with such trepidation is that it assumes there's even a chance that they wouldn't be shitting on our campaign every opportunity they got anyway. Which, as we knew they would, they did.

So I said why not embrace their confrontational, contrarian, condescending stance and turn it around on them. But do it in a way that makes it irresistible for them as well.

You don't have to hate the player. You just have to call out the game. And the more you call out the game, the player is either going to have to defend the game or be ashamed of being a player.

Whenever they tried to call us out for some bullshit, or tried to twist my words into something they definitely were not, or were merely overly aggressive in the service of the status quo, I didn't just answer the question. I answered it with total fucking swagger and then implored them to tell me when they or their network would ever be as forceful with my opponents over issue x, y, and z.

I asked them why the corporate media asks as many tough questions of the powerful as a virgin speed dating with the cast of America's Next Top Model.

I asked them when they were going to drop the facade and just name their show, "He Said She Said."

I asked them why they were reinforcing the rigidity of these political identities. I asked them if they recognized the level of their culpability in beating these labels into our brains, just like they've beat the status quo into our brains. I asked them if they realized that that's the underlying purpose of their job.

And you know what? That shit was hot. Voters loved watching that shit. And, low and behold, the networks loved the ratings.

So I straight up told them. I'll give you your ratings, but you gotta come candid. That's the bargain. You want an interview, you gotta admit shit. Any reporter sitting down with me has gotta acknowledge what color the political sky is. And by that, I mean money fucking green.

None of this sparring for the sake of a fight. Interviewing me was going to be like taking a goddamn political lie detector test, for the reporters. The point being to create enough pressure in the room that it popped their establishment bubble and forced them to fess up to the average voter's reality.

Now, as much as I would like to tell you it worked out that way every time and that we were able to call them out enough they actually adopted our narrative, you and I both know that type of expectation wouldn't have met the threshold for wishful thinking.

Lucky for us, it wasn't about making them propagandists for the Left. Because, the truth is, people don't need forcing leftward. People just need proper information and vibrant debate.

That was the goal. And we were never going to get there if we were always the ones on defense. Our strategy of going on the offense was to make them defend the indefensible until they became so self-conscious they started taking seriously the stakes involved in their contribution.

And in the process of trying to make them humans again, we made their asses stars. Clinically symbiotic, our goals were compatible. We both needed numbers. Ears and eyes. And the ratings we supplied made it a privilege to get my time.

Thus the bargain was struck. We provided wide eyes and dropped jaws, and they provided it right back.

We're Number One?

End of speech for Candidates Forum hosted by College Republicans, Graves College

To believe in American Exceptionalism is either to live in a world where we do not believe in rule of law, a world where rule of law only applies to others and never to us, or it is to live in a world of magic.

It is to live in a world where our foreign policy is nothing but benevolent. It is to live in a world where the military has never been used for anything other than altruism. It is to live in a world where we have never supported tyrants, and only supported democracies. It is to live in a world where business is always out to help the little guy, and the rich take care of the poor. It is to live in a world where a rising tide lifts all boats, and the government has never engaged in acts of sabotage or violence against its own people.

A world of magic. Big dicks and pony rides. That's American Exceptionalism.

Because, remember, it's either that type of exceptionalism or it's being the country that's exceptional for not adhering to even the most basic foundation of morality. The country that believes they can say and do anything they want because *we're* special. And why are we special? Because we say we're special.

Of course, I'm sure some folks would disagree with my take on this. I'm sure there's probably a lot of folks who really do believe that we are exceptional. In that, we're the best. That we're Number One. We're Number One.

But what if you're right? What if we are Number One?

The question then becomes, "What do we do with that?"

If there's one thing I know about Republicans, it's that they can't stand elitists. And they especially hate when the Democrats act like they're better than them. And to be honest, I don't blame 'em. Nobody likes the asshole who acts like he's better than everybody else.

So why in the hell would we let our country be that dude. Because that's what American Exceptionalism is. It's telling the rest of the world that we're hands down better than all of them. That they ain't shit, and we're the only ones who really matter.

Well, I don't want my country to be that dude. In fact, if some jerk said that to me in a bar, I might be tempted to put a couple lumps on his head.

We have to quit acting like that dude. That "We're Number One" shit is played out.

Especially in light of how not Number One we are on so many issues nowadays.

It doesn't mean we don't have the potential to do some truly outstanding things. It doesn't mean we can't be a leader on the world stage. But to do either, we have to be humble and hard working. But more than that, we need friends. We don't need countries who tolerate us because we're waving a gun around. And if we do need that, then maybe we're not as awesome as we think we are.

I believe we can be awesome. But not if we keep engaging in magical thinking. And definitely not if we're acting like that dude.

Let's not go around telling everyone how exceptional we are. Let's prove how good we can be.

Let's not be what we hate. Let's be awesome.

Let's be America.

Note:

Ever since the racism of manifest destiny, the concept of American Exceptionalism has been a cancer on the soul of this nation. If you're not familiar with all the reasons why this is the case, I would encourage you to read William Blum's *Killing Hope*, or (as I've previously pointed out) damn near anything political from Noam Chomsky.

Sadly, most people are not all that familiar with this history, and the only real understanding they have of American Exceptionalism is the belief that We're Number One. And yet for the last at least forty years, outside of the things we really don't want to be Number One at, the only thing we've really been Number One at is thinking We're Number One. That and outspending the military of the five next richest nations combined, which, in terms of

Washington consensus foreign policy, is the only Number One that counts. Ironically, our propensity to make it rain on the military industrial sector, so we can be Number One internationally, comes at the expense of rationing our domestic priorities and becoming a story of unsung potential (compared to our peers internationally).

It's no secret that our Republican brothers and sisters are more overtly expressive of their patriotic sentiment. And, frankly, we weren't sure how it was going to fly when a candidate talked straight about the relative dickishness of American Exceptionalism.

The one thing I did know was that I wasn't about to bore them with a series of lectures on the origins of manifest destiny. This wasn't a matter of information; it was a matter of emotion. So rather than appealing this time to their intellectual honesty, I appealed to their emotional honesty. I told them that I understood that sense of patriotism, the sense of belonging to a larger community. And that the love they had for their country was not that dissimilar to their love for family. But that I also understood that we could be honest about our families and still love them. Each one of us has someone in our family that's done something fucked up. Some of us have a lot of those someones, and some have done things more fucked up than others. But, at the end of the day, we've found a way to still love them. Meaning, if we want it, there is always a path back to love. And there is something about family that makes that path worth it.

Acknowledging the wrongs and missteps within our family doesn't mean we love that family any less. In fact, to not admit those wrongs is to not learn from them. To not get better. To not heal. To never really move forward.

What far too many in the political class have done is to deny our wrongdoing or simply dismiss it with the assumption that we always have the best of intentions. Not only does that keep a country ignorant, but it makes a country arrogant. American Exceptionalism is not just about being Number One; it's about never feeling the need to be self-critical.

This, of course, isn't that rare. Lots of societies believe they're Number One. The point is why being Number One is useful to the powerful. A populace who already believes they are Number One internationally has no reason to pressure their government to be a more just actor on the world stage. A populace who believes they are Number One domestically has little curiosity as to the alternatives in other countries, little reason to fight for something better inside their own. A populace obsessed with being Number One individually is too preoccupied with consumption and thing-based success to ever pursue collective greatness, or even maintain what progress they've achieved.

If we can't talk about ourselves, honestly, we can't be self-critical. We can't see when we're failing, when we're regressing, when we're destructing. Nor can we distinguish our truly great actions from the grand intentions of our folly.

We wouldn't wish such a trait upon a family member, and we shouldn't embrace such a trait in our patriotic ethos.

How We Treat The Stranger

Excerpt from speech delivered to the local Chamber of Commerce

When we talk about Immigration, we must first ask. What is a country?

Is it a language, in our case, a language with its origin in another country? Is it imaginary lines that were drawn and then redrawn and redrawn and redrawn? Is it an arbitrary pattern of colors waved on a stick?

Who we are can't be imitation or imaginary or arbitrary. Who we are, at its core, is how we treat each other. And how we treat each other rests on how we see each other. Our country's worth, our country's beauty, is not a matter of seeing each other as Americans, but seeing each other as humans.

And if we cannot see those among us, whether they be citizens or non-citizens, as humans first, then our language and our borders and our flag are nothing more than the denial of our own humanity.

If there is one measure of a good nation, a just nation, it must be how that nation treats the most vulnerable in its midst. How we treat the least among us. Not based on where they came from, but where they are. Are immigrants and asylum seekers in a just country or are they in an indifferent country?

You and I could have been born anywhere in the world. You and I could have been born into circumstances hard for us to even imagine. Who we become as people is not just a matter of what we do. It is also a matter of how we are treated by others, including and often most importantly when we are the stranger.

The issue of immigration is not how we guard what we were born into. Immigration is how we treat the stranger.

Contrary to what some may argue, I believe that a country is not what is owned; it is what is shared. Just like I believe humanity is not what is owned; it is what is shared.

Our country must be the demonstration of our humanity. In other words, our country is our values. And you cannot own values.

But you can share them. And you share your values by demonstrating them.

When we think of immigration, we must never think in terms of us and them. We must think in terms of who we are, and who we could have been.

When I think of immigration, I think of a man who was a stranger for the most crucial parts of his life. And that man told those who looked up to him, "Whatever you did not do for one of the least of these, you did not do for me."

On any given policy, there may be nuances in which we disagree. But I believe that, when it concerns the strangers who come to us in search of help and/or refuge, we absolutely do agree on the foundational principles that policy must be based upon. And I promise to let those principles guide my vote.

Note:

How do you communicate a progressive stance on immigration to a voting base that has been told for years one of their greatest threats is the criminals and rapists pouring in across our southern border?

For one, you don't start with policy. You start with an understanding. Guiding principles that they have no choice but to acknowledge as true and just. And the ideology they must reject as antithetical to those principles.

For instance, when pressed on my immigration stance in a town hall a few weeks after this speech, I declared, "If you want someone to lie to you, I won't do it. If you want someone to give you hatred, I won't do it.

Anyone who believes in basing one's social standing, privileges, or rights on the coincidence of that person's birth, the unchosen, unearned time and place of their arrival on this planet, might better identify with a system of monarchy or a system of caste or an outright allegiance to white supremacy.

For you certainly don't identify with the type of democracy that, at its dawn, proclaimed as self-evident that all humans were created equal, endowed by their Creator with certain unalienable

Rights. Those, I may remind you, the words of immigrants. The words of men in a land alien to their own ancestry.

If you want someone to sully those words, if you want someone to tar our nation's potential with conditional liberty and arbitrary justice, I won't do it.

You know what 'created equal' means. You know what 'unalienable rights' means. I'm not telling you something you don't already know. I'm telling you not to let my opponents tell you those words don't mean anything anymore."

I'll never know whether these kinds of appeals won hearts and minds or whether they just won me enough benefit of the doubt to get me through the primary. I just know there were certain times on the campaign trail where all I could do was put it out there and trust in the voters. After all, I was expecting them to put a dude like me into office. So what the hell else would I tell them?

Republican Idol

Campaign Ad

The Republican establishment wants you to believe that there's a box you have to fit into if you're going to call yourself a Republican.

But in order for you to believe that, you'd have to forget that Republican President Ronald Reagan signed into law the 1986 Immigration Reform and Control Act, eventually granting amnesty to 2.7 million undocumented immigrants. Not to mention, as a Republican governor, old Ronnie was a staunch supporter of abortion access.

But that's not all?

They also want you to forget that Republican President Richard Nixon created both the EPA and OSHA, called for Universal Health Insurance, and backed a guaranteed income for all Americans. Oh, and did I mention? Tricky Dick instituted racial quotas as federal employment policy and signed the anti-gender discrimination Title IX legislation.

And if that wasn't enough, they really don't want you to remember that Republican President Dwight D. Eisenhower A) denounced the Military Industrial Complex, B) furthered the cause of welfare and unions, and C) oversaw a top marginal tax rate of 91 percent for the richest of Americans.

For God's sake. Republican President William Howard Taft advocated for two or three months of vacation a year.

At one time, the Republican Party was the party of high taxes, big spending, and even bigger regulations.

There is no rulebook that says what a Republican has to be. From Abe to Teddy to Ike, the most famous Republican presidents weren't friends of Industry; they were champions of the worker.

Republican Identity is whatever Republicans want it to be. Whatever you want it to be.

Don't let the Republican Establishment tell you who you have to vote for. Don't let them tell you who you have to be.

My name is H.F. Valentine, and *woooooo* do I approve this message.

Note:

At one time, the GOP was the party of Lincoln, revered by many as the Great Emancipator. Today, the Republican Party is at odds with the slogan "Black Lives Matter." Indeed, some of the most notable Republican presidents in history would have to take a DNA test to prove they were the same species as modern day Republicans.

Yet, with only so much time on the stump, I couldn't expect voters to endure an exploration of how the Party swung from one end of the pendulum to the other. What I had to get across was that the Republican Party is not some statue forever frozen in time. It can change and it can adapt. It can get better and it can get worse.

Republicans are not scolded when they proudly cite the names of Lincoln, Roosevelt, or Eisenhower, two of those three having been immortalized on Mount Rushmore. So I asked why Republicans should feel any reservation voting for a candidate with policies cut from the most favorable patterns of their cloth.

Furthermore, if freedom and liberty were supposed to be the calling cards of the Republican Party, then how in the hell does being a Republican today mean adhering to a strict set of pledges laid out by well-connected power brokers, often completely out of touch with the average voter's daily existence?

While my opponents (and their media allies) were asking if a progressive minded candidate had any business running as a Republican, I was asking Republicans what it even means to be in the GOP.

If there was one question this entire political experiment hinged upon, it was whether my voters saw their political identity as a matter for men like Newt Gingrich and Mitch McConnell to decide, or if it was a matter for them to decide when they were alone in the voting booth.

What's Wrong With Us

Campaign Ad

A half a million homeless. In the richest nation in the world. Libertarians shame them for not making the right choices. Liberals shame you if you use the wrong term to describe the situation.

And yet the real shame is on all of us. What's wrong with us, America?

If someone loses their house, their apartment, their room, you don't leave them to the streets. You give them a place to stay. A decent place to stay.

It's safer for them. It's cheaper for society. And it's the quickest way to get folks back on their feet.

There are millions of vacant hotel rooms, of second homes, of mansions, yachts, and sailboats in the United States

What there are none of is excuses.

My name is H.F. Valentine, and it is a damn shame that I have to approve this message.

Note:

Granted, the issue of homelessness is not what we consider a "sexy" issue. But for anyone who's ever had to spend even one night without a private and safe place to lay your head, you know it's an important one.

Like more issues than we're proud to admit, the solution to this one is pretty goddamn simple. You just give people a place to live, a modest roof to stay under until they can find something better.

It has been tried. It has been proven. And it is the least expensive, most efficient answer.

Unfortunately, this solution is far more controversial than the fact that there are so many Americans homeless in the first place. Hence the question, "What's wrong with us, America?"

Different Degrees Of Family

Excerpt of opening address given at League Of Women Voters Primary Town Hall

You know the only way we, and by we I mean Homo sapiens, were able to survive as a species? Empathy and cooperation. Our connection with one another. And the accumulation of our contributions. That's it. That's the story of humanity. Empathy and cooperation.

That's not to say there weren't rugged individualists a hundred thousand years ago. I'm sure there were. It's just that - they all got eaten.

There wasn't no such thing as a self-made caveman, if you know what I'm saying.

Of course, today's rugged individualists will insist that such talk is nothing more than socialist propaganda, and it eats them up that I won't just spell it out for everyone. In other words, they don't like that I use *other words.* They would prefer that I just come out and say what I mean, what I mean being whatever they can easily twist, tarnish, and demonize.

But here's the thing. What I'm talking about is not what they're talking about. Their definitions are often significantly different from my definitions. And because I know that they're not going to use my definitions, I would rather just speak in terms like empathy and cooperation, and greater economic democracy. It's not that I'm trying to hide anything. It's that I want to be clear about what it is I'm talking about.

Because more and more, it seems like any word you use can be misconstrued and turned against you. For instance, I was accused of being a Stalin-loving communist the other day because I used the words "solidarity" and "collective" in a speech.

Except solidarity is just unity. It's just agreement of feeling, and my willingness to back you up when you're down. Can we no longer express these sentiments? Are these sentiments not your sentiments?

And, my God, collective just refers to teamwork. Is teamwork somehow taboo? Is that where we're at?

I know they want us all to think as individuals, to believe it's every dog for itself. But if there's one thing the average person can appreciate, it's teamwork. And this is evident in the average person's love of sports.

We love some sports. And as sports lovers, we know the value in sports is learning the value of teamwork. To work together toward a common goal. To work for something bigger than yourself. And to at times sacrifice your own shine so others may shine. We learn the virtue of fair play and good sportsmanship. And we realize that if we as a team have done our best, we can hold our head high even in defeat.

That's what teamwork and team spirit is all about.

And guess what? Politics and the facilitation of government is a team sport. Economics is a team sport. Society is a team sport. From a hundred thousand years ago 'til this very day, life is a team sport.

Every bit of progress we hold dear was the product of teamwork. Our roads. Our bridges. Our sanitation networks. Our communication networks. Our schools. Our universities. Our research laboratories. Our libraries. Our societal and economic infrastructure. It's all teamwork. Every technological or artistic achievement, every innovation, every breakthrough resulted from the collective accumulation of innovations and breakthroughs before it.

So whenever you hear my opponents or the media describe me, using scary words like Soooooocialism, just know that what they're referring to is my embrace of teamwork and team spirit. My embrace of empathy and cooperation. My embrace of greater economic democracy.

And know this. When they use these words to scare you, it's because they don't want you to think in terms of teamwork and team spirit. Because if you start thinking in terms of teamwork, you're going to figure out which team you're really on. And if you figure out which team you're really on, you're going to figure out which team they are really on. And let me give you a little hint, it ain't your team.

Because, see, right now they've got too many of us believing that our fellow worker is our competition, that our fellow worker is our opponent. Especially our fellow workers who may not look like us, or who may not have come from the same place as us. They're telling us that "those people" are out to get us, are out to get over on us.

But I'm telling you that those human brothers and sisters are part of your team. And that you share so much more in common with them than you will ever share in common with the ones telling you to be afraid of a candidate like me.

The ones who tell you to be afraid of a candidate like me pit you against your human brothers and sisters so you don't work together toward a common goal. So you don't work for something bigger than yourself. So you don't see your brothers and sisters as a team worth sacrificing for, worth backing up when they're down and they need help.

They tell you to be afraid of this word or that word or this label or that label because it's more acceptable than telling you to be afraid of your human brothers and sisters. But that's what they want. They want you to be afraid. They want you to live with this fear. They want that fear to disorient you. They want you to see the people on your team as a threat. So you will not understand that fighting them, that hurting them, is actually hurting yourself.

As long as I'm in this race, my opponents and the media are going to use these words to try and scare you. They're going to tell you that I'm trying to pull something over on you.

But you know, that when I talk about teamwork and team spirit, that when I tell you that your team is so much bigger than they would have you believe, and that I too am on your team, and that our team can win, I'm not telling you anything you don't already know.

Note:

While some saw it as redundant in a primary, I found there was real value in emphasizing over and over who is and is not on your team.

And let me just say, right off the bat, anyone who is repping this system of inequality is not on your team. Anyone who sells you half measures for life and death problems is not on your team. Anyone who feeds on your fear while simultaneously feeding your fear of the other is not on your team.

But here's the thing. It doesn't matter if you know who the other team is if you *don't know* who is on your team.

There's a reason I used the words brothers and sisters in that speech and throughout my campaign. And that's because we must see each other as what we are. Family.

Now, obviously, I don't mean immediate, all in one household, nuclear family. I mean the kind of family that is born out of struggle. And just as there are different kinds of oppressions, there are different kinds of struggles. Which means there are different degrees of family. But that is ok. My aunt's family is its own unit. But I know that they are also my family and will be there if and when I need them.

Likewise, when black and/or brown people find themselves in a struggle that is unique to them, their white brothers and sisters need to be there to back them up. Because when it comes to the struggle to put food on the table, to afford the rent, to afford medication, to afford tuition, to keep your family safe, we, as working people, are all in the same extended family.

Or let me put it another way. If the people on the other team, the people who *don't* have to worry about those things, consequently the people who have a greater economic and political impact on how these circumstances come about in the first place, would *not* acknowledge Joe or Jane Shmo as one of their own, would *not* see Joe or Jane in the same *class* as them, the same *family* as them, then it would be wise for *you* to recognize Joe and Jane as *your* brother and sister in the struggle.

Because believe me. You may not acknowledge or even know who your family is, who your team is. But the other team, the people who *don't* have to worry about those struggles and who in fact contribute to your own, they most definitely know who is in their family.

There are different degrees of families. There are families within families. And sometimes those families can have major disagreements. But when it comes to the oppression of even one member of that family, we have to be there. We have to act like family act. And show love and support and assistance. You can call it solidarity. You can call it teamwork. I don't give a damn what you call it. As long as you're there for it. That's what matters. Showing the fuck up and knowing who you can count on and who can count on you. That's family. And we need more of it.

Department Of Community

Excerpt from Granger Hills speech for the Fraternal Order of Police

The first thing we have to do is to clarify what our goals are. And I believe it is entirely uncontroversial to suggest that the main goal of a civilized society would be to see as few human beings as possible locked in cages. Now, that may sound elementary. But it's important to state. Because the first step in getting to such a place is to identify the entities within our society that do not share this goal. To identify the operations and institutions that are incentivized to perpetuate mass incarceration, to accelerate mass incarceration.

First and foremost, prison profiteering. We can't even claim to give a fuck about this problem until we get rid of a for profit prison system. And that includes prison food and health services, prison phones and commissary services. It even includes the rental of jails and space to other detention agencies. As long as there is money in locking people up, and that a sliver of that money can find its way to politicians, we ain't gonna do shit about this.

The second thing we have to do is acknowledge the immorality of an economy that relies on prison staff. In some localities, the prison is the biggest employer in town. That's unacceptable. We cannot predicate the survival of one human being on the misery of another.

As we phase out these jobs, we have to make sure there are economic opportunities for those who never wanted this work in the first place. Children don't dream about being a prison guard when they grow up. And we owe it to our children to do better than that.

The next thing we have to do is end the drug war. Prohibition lasted 13 years. The drug war has lasted half a century. It doesn't work. There are models to address addiction that do work. We have to begin looking at the evidence. Giving addicts a criminal record only makes their journey to come home that much farther. Not to mention giving recreational users a criminal record is such an obvious and simultaneously unnecessary net loss for society.

But it's not just drugs. A quarter of the daily jail population is low level offenses. Between fines, bail bonds, court costs, jail time, and probation/parole violations, we have to take a long look at the 13 million misdemeanor charges we dole out every year and what it's costing our society. We have to start thinking about what it is we're using, not just our jails and prisons for, but what we're using our police for. We owe it to the incarcerated, their families, and to those in law enforcement and the courts to test different alternatives.

But what about violence? We gotta do something about violence. And we *do* have to do something. The problem is the disproportionate amount of attention that we have paid toward, the disproportionate amount of salaries we have paid in the service of, merely reacting to violence. And merely reacting to violence is to admit the failure of a society.

Our task should be to prevent violence.

Now, you have programs like the Restorative Justice Diversion Programs that try to intercept harm before it can manifest. And these programs are important. Not only do they have the potential to preempt injury or death, but they also preempt having to call the police. They preempt having to use the courts, having to watch yet another neighbor or family member get locked up. And as these programs develop and spread, I believe they will yield increasingly positive results.

But it's not enough. By the time you have to employ a restorative justice diversion team to prevent violence before it happens, or God forbid to employ a restorative justice process to address violence that has already occurred, it's too late. And I mean too late in the sense that the types of principles that these programs are built upon shouldn't be learned when I'm 20 years old and got beef with somebody. They ought to be taught when I'm five years old, and then six years old, and then seven years old, and so on to when the time I'm 20 and I'm deciding how to settle my disagreement with another human being, violence won't even be a consideration.

These aren't one or two time conversations we should be getting heart-to-heart from a parent or mentor. They are lessons that should be explored over and over in school.

In Denmark, schools have actual empathy classes. In America, schools have mock trials.

If we're going to take these issues on, we have to get serious about what that's going to entail. And what that's going to entail is us looking at each other differently.

When we see our neighbor for their capacity to do wrong, we invest our resources in police and courts and jails and prisons. But what if we truly saw our neighbor for their capacity for good? What would we be investing in if we expected to develop and nurture that good?

We have to quit thinking in terms of reacting.

And that's why when I enter the United States Congress I plan to sponsor a bill that does away with the Department of Homeland Security, a department that by its very nature is reactionary, and instead redirect those funds into a new Department. The Department of Community. A Department that coordinates and facilitates the testing of proposed alternatives for education and social investment, that tests initiatives to eradicate addiction, hunger and homelessness, that gathers evidence and promotes the policies, both economic and social, that are proven to reduce the need for law enforcement, the courts, and incarceration.

I believe these types of policies, these types of programs, this type of investment will build stronger individuals. But even the most resilient individuals need community. And community requires investment, it requires development, it requires nurturing. And if we don't see the communities around us for all the potential they have to offer, neither will we see our own as individuals.

I want you to imagine if an enemy of the state were to pull off a plan, kidnapping 2 million of our citizens and holding them hostage in cages for just one night. Can you even imagine what our response would be? From the CIA to the FBI to the Department of Homeland Security, we would spare absolutely no expense in our response?

But I ask you, what good are all those agencies, what good is a Department of Homeland Security, when it's the homeland perpetrating the abduction?

Our security doesn't call for more prisons or more judges or more badges. It calls for more community.

Note:

While reforms in the criminal justice system are immediately necessary, we must be revolutionary minded and see all related policy through the lens of reducing the need for that system in the first place.

When it comes to incarceration and our criminal justice system's quite unjust results, I think, like most of our societal problems, the issue rests on how we are not allowed to look at the world. And when we are not encouraged to think of problems in terms of systems and institutions, when we are not encouraged to think of our connection to a diverse and necessary community, is it any wonder how easy we make it to just blame individuals?

Moreover, I would suggest it is the very existence of the law and order beast that compels us to continue feeding that beast, if for no other reason than it was us who created it.

But just because we find ourselves in a hole doesn't mean we have to keep digging. Even if you don't see the way we have counterintuitively designed these institutions to be the main problem, you have to at least acknowledge that counterintuitive design as being a catalyst.

Since a campaign speech doesn't allow you to get too deep into the weeds, I merely alluded to the broad concept of education and social investment as part and parcel of achieving a community centered solution. Yet I would also include the prisons themselves in this broader view of community. As shamefully easy as it's been for us to close the door on prisoners and no longer see them as part of society, our broader success and security depends on the success of our confinement facilities being truly rehabilitory, and not merely punitive.

Of course, like so much of this solution, that would put the focus on systems and institutions rather than on people. And that is something policymakers are often loath to do, especially when they don't have solutions, especially when they have donors who rely on us not finding a solution.

Lucky for us, my campaign didn't spend one second dancing for donors. Our appeal was to the voter. While my opponents centered their policy proposals on how to best react once the harm had been done, we centered on prevention and the inherent safety of strong communities.

During a primary debate, I told my opponents that all their big talk about deterrence, which if we're honest is just code for revenge, may get loud applause and flapping jaws at rallies. But, in the long term, voters have to look at what it really means in their lives.

Then I looked out into the audience and asked, "What would you really prefer? Not in a soundbite, not in a momentary burst of emotion. But what reality would you prefer to live under?

A society less equipped to prevent violent crime and more equipped to harden a person before they come out of prison? Or a society that preempts most violent crime and minimizes recidivism for those who come out of actual rehabilitation facilities?

I could talk big talk too, but it's not going to provide you any more freedom or any more safety. The freedom and safety of individuals relies on the design of the community within which those individuals reside. We can damn each other with suspicion and turn all among us into potential enemies. Or we can recognize ourselves as human family and prepare a society worthy of family.

I've made my choice. Now you gotta make yours."

A Sinner Nonetheless

Excerpt from impromptu press conference outside Madison Square Karaoke

You have to love how my opponents spent so much of their lung space hooting and hollering about PC culture, then even more hooting and hollering about cancel culture. But then I come along, shake things up a little bit, and all the sudden they're clutching pearls that don't even belong to them. They're rifling through the Identity Politics Manual of Liberal Karate like it's scripture before a bible verse contest. They're out here getting triggered, catching the vapors, and doing their very best imitation of the very worst of the social justice warriors they criticized for the last decade.

Sadly, it's not enough for me to point out how hypocritical it is, how disingenuous it is, how utterly desperate it is. No. I've got to address the attacks. Because the 24 hour a day, 7 day a week, 365 day a year, self-appointed judge, jury, and executioners on Twitter, or as I like to call it "the Cleversphere," demand such.

So I *will* address it. But I'll address it on my own terms. And my terms are to recall a joke that the great Bill Hicks told one time. And the joke went that three rednecks came up to him after a show and said, "Hey, Mr. Funny Man. Come here. We're Christians, and we don't like what you said." And Bill responded, "Then forgive me."

And that's exactly what I'm asking you.

In fact, this whole campaign is the campaign of a sinner trying his best to be redeemed.

And I know what some of you are thinking. "But H.F., how can you say that? You're not even a believer."

And that is true. But I am a sinner nonetheless. And I come from a tradition of sinners finding their way and then giving their testimony so others might find their way. That's what I'm doing. I'm just not doing it in the religious sphere; I'm doing it in the political sphere.

As someone who sat in the pews, who sat in Chapel, who read the Bible, who studied the Bible, and then moved forward holding onto the most precious elements of that story, I understand what it means to ask forgiveness for your sins. I understand the seeking of redemption. And not just for the one or two bad things I've been called out on in this pathetic attempt by my opponents, but for all the bad things I may have done in my life. For any time I hurt someone or took another human being for granted and acted in my own selfish interest, I have committed the rest of my life to trying to make up for those sins.

That's why I'm running for this office. And the authority that I am running on is the person I used to be. The sinner who saw the error of his ways and who made it his mission to take what little gifts he had and contribute to the making of a better world, not just for some people, but for all of us, and for all who come after us.

So when they point out my past, all they're really doing is allowing me once again to bear witness. To give sincere testimony that we don't have to stay the same person. That we as a people don't have to stay the same people. And that our politics don't have to stay the same politics.

Now, if I can't get an Amen to that, it means we're all out of Amens.

Note:

I've never hid the fact that I had a sketchy-ass past. In fact, I used to be what I would consider *kind of a piece of shit*. And as I've tried to become a better person and find a way to contribute to a better world, I've thought a lot about how my past actions factor into those efforts and the limits they may place on those efforts.

Luckily, someone running in a GOP primary has less worry of getting called out for past transgressions than someone in a Democratic primary, especially for the kind of sins I myself have been guilty of. However, don't think for a second that the Republicans were above such an attack. Once I started to gain real traction with voters, it was a given they would drag out the Oppo Research. *Even though* a couple of my opponents were still currently engaged in the same behavior.

This kind of scrutiny, in the Republican Party, is only ever aimed at someone who is seen to be upsetting the Republican donor applecart. And the only way I could see to defend against such an attack was to appeal directly to the voters, using a language the voters were familiar with.

First, to remind them how much my opponents bellyached about the Democrats and cancel culture, only then to co-opt their performative wokeness the moment voters figured out these aspiring leaders had showed up to the party empty headed.

And second, to claim the title of sinner. Repentant and reflective. All in the hopes that they themselves would appreciate this sentiment and would actually help make the case for my redemption, just as many of them had sought their own.

Both of which kept with the slogan "I'm not telling you anything you don't already know." I can't stress enough how important this ethos was to my campaign.

Not only was it honest, but it was efficient. You cannot lecture your way into office. Most voters will take someone trying to educate them as condescension. That's why nine times out of ten, a populist will beat a professor. And the tenth time, the professor was a populist.

Crowds don't want to be corrected; they want to be agreed with. In other words, they want to be met where they are at. And my only real shot was to clean the propaganda off of what they already knew to be true and ask them very nicely to keep that truth clean until Election Day.

No More

Campaign Ad

For every family who's lost a loved one to incarceration in this war.
For every family who's lost a loved one to violence in this war.
For every family who's lost a loved one to overdose in this war.
For anyone listening who lost someone they loved in this war, there's only one question.
Was this war worth losing the one you loved?
War is a choice. And it's time for us to make the right choice and end this one.
No more corners. No more cartels.
No more fear of asking for help. No more hiding in the shadows.
No more neighborhoods kept down. No more families devastated.
No more war.
No more war.
No more drug war.

My name is H.F. Valentine, and I wholeheartedly approve this message.

Note:

In 1971, Republican President Richard Nixon began the "war on drugs" in the interest of destroying the anti-war left and black people. According to John Ehrlichman, Nixon's aide on domestic affairs at the time, criminalizing marijuana was meant to disrupt the hippies, and criminalizing heroin was meant to disrupt the black community. With a constant assault of arrests and raids, the mission was to "vilify them night after night on the evening news."

John Ehrlichman, an aide to the President who started the drug war, was quoted saying, "Did we know we were lying about the drugs? Of course we did."

Now, even if you're someone who doesn't believe that, and faithfully believes that the drug war was really about public health, I believe the last half a century of this war has proven beyond the shadow of a doubt that, as it pertains to public health, it is a colossal failure.

The problem is that the drug war has become institutionalized, and has been a colossal success for arms manufacturers, the prison industry, and anyone else who profits off this misery machine. Any attempt to end this war is going to bring out every asshole skilled enough to feed you propaganda with one hand and count their bribes with the other.

That's why my ad wasn't about statistics. It was about stories. And almost everyone in this country has a loved one they've lost, in one way or another, to the drug war.

My constituents have heard all the propaganda. They've been bombarded with it for decades. What they haven't been bombarded with is the evidence-based solutions that could have saved the one they loved.

It wasn't a problem that my voting audience had historically been the greatest supporters of the war on drugs. It was a gift. I've heard both addicts and those who've buried addicts say they would never wish that upon another soul. The policies I offered those people were ones of hope. Something which is wholly absent in the drug war.

If we can spread that hope and push voters to expect something different, we may just have a shot at turning the tide in Washington. It won't be quick, and it won't be pretty. Selling the radical policies it will take to bring about the drug war's conclusion is no doubt an uphill climb.

But what else is there really to do? Haven't we been going downhill long enough?

I'm Not Afraid Of Who We Are

Excerpt from Interview with Brad Bailey, Fox News

Mr. Valentine, you are getting a lot of press, and your polling is significantly higher than was expected at the beginning of your campaign. But do you really think what you're saying is resonating with voters, or is it just about the spectacle of your run for office?

Listen to what you're asking. Your assumption is that the voters are idiots. That they're not capable of being genuinely engaged; they're only capable of being entertained.

That's not what I'm saying. I'm saying that, by all previous standards, it's a stretch to believe GOP voters are going to take you seriously enough to actually cast their ballot for you when Election Day comes.

Maybe that's because the previous standards you're referring to don't take the voters seriously.

Just look at the way the average voter, the average citizen, is treated by their various spheres of influence. And I'm not just talking about Republican voters; I'm talking about everybody.

Whether it's business, the workplace, politicians, news and media organizations, even religious operations, far too many of these actors would prefer that we not develop too much critical thinking skills.

Well, that sounds a little conspiratorial.

It's not conspiratorial. I don't even think it's all that controversial.

You just have to look at the interests of these actors. In which situation are they going to fare better? When we're accustomed to taking orders, or when we're constantly asking questions about our own self-determination? When we're so easily persuaded, or when we can easily recognize propaganda and false arguments?

Obviously, they would prefer us going with the flow. In fact, I would go as far as to say that they're actually afraid of what might happen if people were left to a lifestyle of more free and open thinking.

Afraid of what?

Afraid of who they might become. If people start challenging the status quo, if people start challenging institutions, if the average person starts asking, starts imagining, what alternatives might look like? That's some scary shit to the jokers in power.

But, see, I'm not afraid of who people might become. Because I'm not afraid of who they really are. I have faith in our humanity, as long as our humanity is nurtured.

And that's what I'm trying to demonstrate in this campaign.

I want people to think for themselves. I want people to ask questions they wouldn't normally ask, questions that challenge conventional wisdom.

When I say to voters I'm not telling them something they don't already know, I'm basically just reminding them of what our core values are, what our shared values are, when they are free from unjust or corrupt influences.

And what makes you think you know what those core values are?

I know what they are because it's the most glaring irony in our society. Our core values are those first few lessons we teach our children, despite them being antithetical to the world we live in.

Antithetical in what way?

In the way that we teach our children not to lie, but our political leaders lie all the time. Hell, advertising and public relations are the art of lying.

We teach our children not to steal, while wages are stolen by our very employers to the tune of 15 billion dollars a year.

We teach our children to share, we teach our children to have respect, we teach our children that it's not if you win or lose but how you play the game. Does that sound at all like the world we live in?

Then why do we do it?

Because we want to believe they'll be better than us. We give them these lessons, this ethical foundation, in the secret hopes that they'll have the courage to do the things we didn't.

The only problem with this kind of thinking is that we're not the only influence in our children's lives. And unless we take the power we have as adults to change those institutions of influence, waiting for the next generation to magically just be better is always going to lead to disappointment.

Every bit of progress we've made has been when enough people admitted that our institutions didn't reflect our humanity, and then did something about it. Something to correct it.

But that takes the freedom to ask questions. This campaign is about that freedom. I tell voters, "You have that capacity. I want to appeal to your intellect. They want to appeal to the side of you that doesn't ask questions."

They want a consumer minded voter, taking orders. I want a citizen voter, critically examining what options are or should be available and then *giving* the orders.

Mr. Valentine, that's a pretty tall order. We only have about a minute left. The question remains to be seen if Republican voters are ready for this much change in their party. What do you say to those who doubt that's the case?

I say that we can't wait for someone else to do it. And neither can we wait for the next generation to do it.

I want to appeal to people's intellect and sense of humanity. I'm not afraid of who we are. That's why my other main slogan is let's get money out of politics and see what happens. Because I have faith in us. And this campaign is a demonstration of that faith.

Thank you for your time, Mr. Valentine.

Thank you for yours.

Note:

I have found, over the many years I have engaged with political conservatives, your only shot at earning serious consideration for a progressive message is if you first commit to taking *them* seriously. And taking them seriously means, at the very least, appealing to that person's intellect and sense of humanity.

Now, I know what a lot of you are thinking. You're thinking there's not a lot of intellect or sense of humanity in *any* of our politics. And I would not necessarily disagree with that. But that is precisely why my campaign was seen as a breath of fresh air.

One of the reasons why there's so much political theater is because politicians don't trust the voters. Therefore, they have to fool them. They have to propagandize them. And very often, they turn them into something they're really not.

While it's obvious I wasn't above political theater myself, my own preference for political theater was to turn off the spotlight and bring all the lights up in the auditorium. To show them that *they* are the real actors. To illuminate their hunger, their hopes, and their dreams. To show them that *they* are the ones who decide the direction of the drama.

To share with them my story of a better world and then put my trust in theirs. And to then leave them with these words: "You don't have to be the voters they see you as. You don't have to abide by these labels, these political identities. You can be and do and vote whatever is in your hearts."

Then Show Love

Excerpt from address to the Hartsdale Rotary Club

"I don't care what they do. I just don't want to see it."

"I don't really have a problem with it. I just don't like when they throw it in my face."

"I love everybody. I just think they can keep it to themselves."

How many times have you heard someone say something like that? How many times have you said it?

I've said it.

I was as homophobic as every other boy I grew up with. I'm of an age where I didn't even know transgender was a thing.

That is to say I have struggled with these issues, and it was a much longer journey for me to get where I am today than I would like to admit.

But it's the truth.

Like all the personal growth in my life, I owe a great deal to the questions I was finally willing to ask. But it wasn't until I befriended and was befriended by members of the LGBTQ community that I was able to ask those questions.

Now, I'm not saying we have to see eye to eye on policy here. What I do have to do though is provide you the basis for my policy. Lucky for me, I don't believe I have to school any of you on the Golden Rule.

And lucky for you, you already have an example of how they "do unto you."

See, we may not always make the effort to get to know our LGBTQ brothers and sisters. But for them, it ain't really a choice. We're everywhere. They can't avoid our asses.

And let's be honest here. Let's be totally honest.

Take a moment and just think about how you feel. If, for whatever reason, something about LGBTQ folks just doesn't sit right with you, I want you to examine why that is.

For some of us, it has to do with a personal fear. An insecurity about ourselves. For some of us, it has to do with our devotion to a strict definition of masculinity or femininity. For some of us, it has to do with the fear for our children. For the hard time they might face if they found themselves in the same world we can't bring ourselves to understand.

Well, here's the thing. LGBTQ people can see that. They can see all that. Because it's plainly written all over our faces.

And if they can see that and feel it coming off us, and they can still give us the benefit of the doubt, they can still see the humanity in us and give us a chance to prove that we're more than our attitudes on this subject? Well, that takes love.

Do you hear what I'm saying? They love us. We're they're neighbors, we're their co-workers, we're their family, we're often even their church family. And they love us.

And the amount of love, the amount of civility, the amount of benefit of the doubt they have shown us is because they know we're worth it, and that there's nothing *inherently* different in us, outside of the difference that *we* can't seem to fully get over.

In the spirit of the Golden Rule, all my policy asks is that you offer them what they've offered you for all these years. And that is love, despite our disagreements.

I don't want to go too deep into preacher mode, but I know for many of us, at some time in our lives, maybe even now, our unease with or opposition to LGBTQ folks has been of a religious nature.

And if that is the case for you, I would simply ask you to pay attention to how you treat the stranger. Not strangers in the sense that you *don't* have people in your social sphere that are LGBTQ. But that sometimes we have people in our lives that might as well be strangers, because we refuse to acknowledge who they are.

It doesn't have to be this way. You have it in you to treat the stranger the way Jesus of Nazareth suggested you treat the stranger. And if you do that, before long, they won't be strangers anymore. They'll be loved ones.

When I was a young man, I thought I knew all I needed to know about "those people." And yet I'd never had a real conversation with someone who I knew was LGBTQ. I'd never listened to their story. I'd never listened to what they wanted out of life.

If you want to understand my policies, you don't need to listen to me as much as you need to listen to them. I'm asking you to do that. The same as I've asked you to listen to me, the same as I have listened to you.

Listen to the stranger. Whether they're LGBTQ or from any other group that just doesn't, for whatever reason, sit right with you. Some of these reasons you may not want to admit. Some of the reasons you may have not come to terms with yet. But whatever the reason, it doesn't change the reality that it is often us, ourselves, who are keeping so many of our brothers and sisters strangers, when they don't have to be.

I'm not saying it's easy. But it surely hasn't been easy for them.

As much as we tell ourselves we embrace the Golden Rule, many of us have a hard time putting ourselves in certain shoes. I, myself, am still working on it, to make sure that the questions I have are out of good faith curiosity and not self-fulfilling prophecy. To make sure I'm doing what I can to make the world a more welcoming place for those who have far too long been *made* to feel like the stranger.

I do this out of love. And yes, sometimes, that love takes time, and work.

But you *can* love. And you can accept love. And once you start to listen, once you start to get to know your brothers and sisters, once you start to see the love that has been given you, it makes it easier to accept that love. And it makes it easier to start giving it back.

If you believe in a God of love, then show love.

If you believe that all humans are created equal, then show your humanity.

We don't have to hate. We don't have to hurt. We don't have to be strangers.

Note:

As much as I enjoy putting on the occasional preacher party, in this speech I probably used more religious language than I would have liked. But what can I say? I grew up in the church. I know how much biblical instruction contributed to my homophobia, and I know how many other lessons there are in the Bible that could have been used to do the opposite.

Did it come off to some as hypocritical, maybe even blasphemous? I'm sure. But the truth is we all cherry pick. And I wagered that voters would comprehend what to take with them and what to leave behind.

And, if I'm totally honest, this speech was as much for me as it was for them. A chance to deliver the sermon I wish I'd been delivered when I was a child and needed it the most.

I hope those who follow in my primary footsteps are able to come up with a better tactic.

A First Amendment Issue

Address to Stuben Ridge Pro-Life Voters Town Hall

One of the first campaign events I held, a voter came up to me afterwards and asked me a question that I think is probably on a lot of your minds. And that is: How could they vote for me as a Christian conservative Republican if I do not share the same stance as them on abortion?

And I told them that it didn't matter what my stance was on abortion. That it didn't amount to a hill of beans what my position was on the issue, because A) I am running for a federal office and all the relevant abortion legislation is state based, B) one vote in the House isn't going to make a difference one way or the other when it comes to a constitutional amendment, and C) House members don't vote on Supreme Court Justices and the Supreme Court is already stacked with justices who see abortion as an abomination. So whatever beliefs I hold on the subject are pretty much a moot point as it pertains to the practical application of law and law enforcement on this issue.

So, for all intents and purposes, my views on the subject are irrelevant. It just doesn't matter what I think.

And, of course, I thought this was a pretty good answer to their question. Until they responded, "That isn't good enough."

And when I asked them why, and when I listened to what they had to say, I agreed with them that that was not a good enough answer. And that there was a whole lot more listening I needed to do, and thinking I needed to do, if I expected Republican voters, many of whom see themselves as single issue voters, to put an X next to my name on their ballot.

So I took that voter to lunch, and while we were eating I asked them if they couldn't vote for me as a Republican or if they couldn't vote for me as a Christian. And they said, "Both."

So I thought about it, and I said, "Well, let's take 'em one by one. Let's start with your vote as a Republican."

Because see, traditionally, Republicans were not opposed to abortion. Until the 1970s, Republicans and Democrats did not have a split along party lines when it came to abortion. In fact, in 1967 then

Governor Ronald Reagan signed a bill into law loosening abortion restrictions. And it wasn't just Reagan either. Barry Goldwater supported abortion rights. Early on, both Senator Prescott Bush and his son George H. W. Bush supported abortion rights. To the point that they were supporters of Planned Parenthood. Hell, President Dwight D. Eisenhower served as Planned Parenthood's honorary co-chair in the 1960s. As late as the 1976 Republican National Convention, public opinion polls were showing Republican voters as being more pro-choice on average than Democrats. At that time, not even half the Party saw themselves as anti-abortion, much less considered this to be an important issue at all.

So what happened? It wasn't that the move to embrace an anti-abortion stance as a party was a matter of principle. It was a political calculation to garner more votes among Democratic voting Catholics. That was the play. And when they saw that this strategy was even more effective with protestant and evangelical social conservatives, the Party decided to exploit this issue.

So much so that now Republican voters see it as part of their political identity. So much so that the person breaking bread with me couldn't see themselves voting for me.

And when I told them this history, I asked them if knowing this made any difference in the way they thought about it. And they were straight with me and told me that they didn't know that history and that they were surprised to hear some of it. But that it wouldn't change their mind. Because the history they were ultimately concerned with went a little bit farther back.

And at that point I had a choice to make. I could try and play a game of "what about this scripture, what about that scripture" and try to add what I believed to be nuance and clarification to their understanding of what the Bible actually has to say on the subject of abortion. Or I could try and make a case for all the issues that would by any stretch of the logical imagination be considered a pro-life issue yet are illogically sacrificed in the name of this single issue.

But then it hit me. Those are terrible ideas. For had I tried either of those tactics, I would have only been arguing with what they saw as their religious conviction. And, from my experience, it makes zero political sense to argue over a stance of faith.

So what I did instead was embrace their stance. I told them I appreciated them acknowledging this was a cornerstone of their religious belief. And that I was not going to argue with that belief.

Moreover, I too thought the Roe v. Wade decision of 1973 was a flawed decision. Not so much that I don't believe the fourteenth, fifth, and possibly ninth amendments' implication of privacy apply to health/medical situations. But rather I thought the case should have ultimately been decided on First Amendment grounds.

The decision in Roe V. Wade talked about the lack of consensus on when life begins. But those who see abortion as an abomination don't really believe it's a matter of life; they believe it's a matter of the soul. Those opposing abortion are not literally pro-life; they're pro-soul. And anyone who would argue with that has to forever part ways with the pepperoni on their pizza.

You know what I'm saying?

Christians don't come to Red Lobster for the ceremonial facilitation of the all you can eat popcorn shrimps' ascension into heaven; they come for the cheddar biscuits. In other words, the Christians I'm talking about don't believe animals go to heaven. And they don't believe animals go to heaven because they don't believe animals have souls. Therefore, those Christians don't believe the taking of life is off limits; they believe the taking of a soul is off limits. And, in their view, the soul is exclusive to the human. Otherwise, half the country would be saying Thanksgiving Day grace over a ten pound tofurkey, and Bikers for Jesus would have to settle for wearing pleather.

Now, I know this may be a strange way to make my case, but if the pro-life stance is really one concerning the soul, and that stance is informed by one's religious faith, then I can no more pledge to legislate according to this Christian belief than I would legislate away the eating of pork or shellfish or, dare I say, outlaw the polycotton blend T-shirt.

And I'll put it to you the same way I put it to my lunch companion. I asked. Would you expect me to fight against bills proposing we encode Sharia Law into Us Law? Would you expect me to fight against bills mandating that the Torah or Vedic Law supersede US Law? Would you expect me to fight against that?

If the answer is yes, you cannot expect me to legislate a matter of the soul. Nor should you want me to.

I can pledge to stand for the religious freedom guaranteed you under the First Amendment. But I cannot pledge to advocate that any religious belief become the law of the land. And that is in your interest as much as anyone else's.

And to make an exception in this case would be to open the door to other religious exceptions down the road, many of which my Christian constituents may not be so happy with.

And after I said all that, we had a talk about the policies I'm pushing in my platform and how they would benefit from those policies. And then we had a talk about how many shitty things Republicans are able to get away with based solely on their anti-abortion stance.

And then I reminded them that as a federal House Rep I would have virtually no impact on the legality or lack of concerning abortion. And neither would my opponent.

So, in reality, their vote in this primary is not about abortion. It's about what difference can actually be made on all these other issues. And that is the reason my opponents will try so hard to get them to focus on abortion and *not* on our other differences.

It's not that I want to avoid the issue of abortion. It's that I want to focus on what I can do. I want to spotlight all the things Republican voters have needed a Republican Representative to actually fight for but haven't seen any fight since the days before their party decided to exploit abortion as a single issue wedge.

And then I put my napkin down on my plate and asked them if I could have their vote.

And you know what they said?

They said, "I'll think about it."

And I tell you, folks, those have to be the sweetest words I've heard since I've been on this campaign. Because that is all I can ask for. And it's all I'm asking of you.

I want you to think about taking a chance. Give me one term. If you think I'm a threat to your values after that one term, vote me out in the next election.

But if you can see my potential as a fighter and you think it might just be worth putting me in the ring to fight for you, then I'm asking you to commit to thinking about it.

Note:

When I initially told people I was thinking about running, the first thing everyone said was, "How in the hell are you going to sell a lefty candidate to Republicans, many of whom may be abortion-minded single issue voters?"

To which, I responded, "Easy. I'll just turn them into a different kind of single issue voter, the new issue being corruption and the necessity to get money out of politics."

And while my answer may have been slightly facetious, I did set out to highlight all the issues that are sacrificed when we don't do anything about money in politics. Not coincidentally, these are most all the same issues that are sacrificed when abortion is the single issue Republicans cast their ballot on.

And while some on the left may think it's selling out to not advocate more forcefully for abortion rights, indeed to try and persuade GOP voters to give up their anti-abortion stance altogether, I think that misses the point of why I was running. The same way we should not legislate religious beliefs, I don't see the sense in trying to use a political campaign to change religious beliefs.

We can't think in terms of who we want people to be. We have to think in terms of anticipated consequences. By spotlighting the fact that abortion is not ingrained in the fabric of the Republican Party, by painting the issue as a First Amendment cause upholding religious freedom, and by driving home the reality concerning just how little of an impact a House Rep has on the issue to begin with, I at least had a shot at getting folks to consider making that exception.

As far as I see it, that's really all you can do. Get them to make the exception. Furthermore, if we can convince single issue voters that making this exception is not sacrificing their views on abortion, then how could we possibly see it as sacrificing our own?

Are there other strategies that could prove more effective? Absolutely. But the only way we're going to know that is if the lefties reading these words try their own runs in Republican primaries.

Not Always Your Friend, Not Always Feminist

Excerpt from speech at Jones Farm Bike Rally

The other day I was being interviewed about drug policy, and out of nowhere the reporter blurts out, "Do you consider yourself a feminist?"

And I said, "You know, I'm really disappointed in you. If you're going to ask a gotcha question, I expect more out of you than that. Obviously I'm a feminist, dumbass. What kind of self-disrespecting ratings chaser are you?

Asking someone if they're a feminist is like asking someone if they're anti-racist. It's kind of a gimme. You need to work on your candidate sabotage game, son."

Of course, we all know why they sprung that on me. They sprung it on me because I'm running in a Republican primary, and the word "feminist" doesn't always leave the best taste in the mouths of conservatives.

But that is because the term feminist has been cast like glass into the same disingenuous fire as terms like Black Lives Matter or antifa or socialist, or liberal or conservative, or hell even Democrat and Republican. When a word is misconstrued or misrepresented or maligned or even co-opted to the point where there's rarely even agreement on what it means, it loses its meaning altogether.

Furthermore, the worst thing that ever happened to the term feminist is that it got relegated to only one side of the political aisle. And that is not an accident.

It is completely uncontroversial to say that the right wing used feminism as a smear against prominent women in the Democratic Party. Yet the ironic thing is not that those same Democratic women welcomed that label and then wore it as a badge of honor. The ironic thing is that many of them counted on that badge to be a shield against what little criticism the mainstream media aimed at their many unfeminist endeavors.

See, Diane Feinstein was a feminist when she was advocating for women's equal pay. But when she was war profiteering from an invasion and occupation that left a million people dead, maybe not so much.

Nancy Pelosi is most definitely acting under feminist principles when she fights for women's reproductive health. But when she ditched the public option, refused to even entertain passage of Medicare for All, and in effect guaranteed an excess of 60,000 unnecessary deaths a year, that was not very feminist of her.

When Hillary Clinton fought for children's health programs domestically and women's rights and women leadership internationally, those were certainly feminist undertakings. But when First Lady Hillary Clinton pushed less assistance for poor women and more incarceration for the young black men she called "super predators," when Senator Hillary Clinton led the Democrats' support for the immoral, illegal, and catastrophic Invasion of Iraq, and Secretary of State Hillary Clinton ensured a successful coup in Honduras and was the most influential voice advocating for the bombing of Libya? Well, let's just say she must have misplaced her what-would-a-feminist-do bracelet those particular days.

The point being, that a lot of our so-called feminist icons in the Democratic Party are not always your friend, not always your enemy, and not always feminist. They're more like the frenemies of feminism. They're freminists or frenemists or freneminists. Use whichever one you like; I've trademarked all three.

And before any good white liberals accuse me of mansplaining feminism to women, I should just point out. It's not mansplaining; it's hackery. Because all I'm doing is just repackaging what other women, many women of color, have been saying for a long long time. Unless that is you would like to whitesplain to black feminists what the real work of feminism is. Oh, that's right. I see your mansplain, and I raise you a whitesplain.

Contrary to what the campaign consultants who conjured up the feminism exploiting trope of the Bernie Bro would have you believe, feminism and feminist policy making is more than just add rich, connected women Democrats and stir.

Whether it's the government, the military, the church, industry, or society as a whole, feminism is more than women's faces in high places.

And it is absolutely NOT finding more women to supervise the status quo.

Having said that, it is important for me to point out what else feminism is not.

Feminism is not anti-men.

It is not anti-religion.

It is not anti-humor.

It is not anti-family or anti-marriage or anti-heterosexuality.

Feminism is not the bogeyman.

Feminism is not something to be afraid of.

Feminism is not coming for your balls.

I've been a feminist for quite some time, and every time I check, they're still there.

In fact, if we recognize balls as a synonym for courage, and we acknowledge that real feminism requires the courage to stand up against the status quo, I don't think it's at all inaccurate to say that feminism takes balls.

It may be ironic and a tad inappropriate to say that, but not inaccurate.

Throughout history, feminists have been nothing if not courageous. And the courage that real feminism requires is born out of love and a radical thirst for justice. And that radical thirst for justice is why I love feminism.

I love feminism for the same reason I love the teachings of Dr. Martin Luther King Jr. Dr. King taught us, "True compassion is more than flinging a coin to a beggar; it comes to see that an edifice which produces beggars needs restructuring."

In that same spirit, feminism is more than a mere response to domestic violence. It is about addressing the institutions and the beliefs that contribute to the making of an abuser, so that we as a society can stop producing abusers.

Is that not a goal that both women and men, Democrat and Republican, can get behind?

The goal of feminism is not to make the police more feminine, to make the military more feminine. It's to make a world with less paths to crime, a world that needs less military.

Is that not a goal that both women and men, Democrat and Republican, can get behind?

Feminism ain't trying to limit your freedoms. It's trying to maximize our fairness.

Feminism ain't about your good intentions. It's about our good consequences.

Feminism ain't being soft. It's being flexible enough to change.

Is that not something both women and men, Democrat and Republican, can get behind?

I know that Republicans hate hearing a Democrat badmouth what they believe it means to be a Republican. I get that. I understand why that would make Republicans resentful of Democrats.

That's why I urge Republicans skeptical of feminism to not make the same mistake.

And don't let someone else do it either. When you hear some talking head tell you that feminists are your enemies, or that feminism is just for those people and not for you. Don't believe them. Don't listen to that shit.

Feminism is not for the high and mighty or the highfalutin. Neither is feminism just for celebrities or academics. And I cannot overstate this next one. Feminism is not just for Democrats.

But most of all, feminism is not just for women.

It's for all of us. All of us who value the life, the liberty, and the pursuit of happiness for a woman - the same as for a man - the same as for anyone.

That's where we have to start, no matter our political affiliation. And that's where feminism starts. A Declaration of Independence and a recognition that we are all created and thus deserving to be treated as equals.

Now, that doesn't mean that all feminists are in lock step on every issue before them. There are disagreements far and wide within the feminist community. And you may not always agree with each and every prevailing feminist stance.

But ask yourself? Are you really supportive of each and every policy platform of the Republican Party?

Hell, nah.

Truth be told, if the Republican Party spent even a fraction of the time listening to what matters to their voters' everyday lives as it spends trying to distract and scare voters with these bullshit labels, they wouldn't have to worry so much about the candidacy of a badass feminist like myself.

So you can ask me that gotcha question any time you want. Because the answer is always going to be the same.

"Hell, yeah, I'm a feminist. And my suspicion is you are too."

Note:

Not only did I embrace the f-word, but I also touted feminism's influence on my policies. While I viewed strategy in this campaign through the lens of wanting to win, I did not want to win bad enough that I had to lie to voters about who I was. It was our transparency, just as much as our audacity, that made it worth voters taking a campaign like this seriously.

One of the things I believed was crucial in this task was getting people to dissociate feminism from certain famous persons or politicians, some of whom they may see as full of shit, and instead to get them to think about feminism in terms of its potential value to society. I gently reminded folks about the progress and achievements we've accumulated due to causes and movements that were undoubtedly feminism inspired and guided. Then I not-so-gently trumpeted feminism's forward-mindedness and practicality in tackling serious issues in the present and into the future.

For instance, while basic human rights ought to be low hanging fruit, its material demonstration is far from a reality. Take violence for example. Our desire for less violence is not just a matter of conscience. According to UN Women, the total estimated cost of violence globally for the year 2015 was $13.6 trillion. Meaning we have both moral and quantifiable grounds upon which to champion feminist solutions.

The problem is that most establishment Democrats stake their feminist credibility on the very lowest hanging of human rights fruits, and the majority of Republican politicians and pundits have conditioned voters to either roll their eyes or get on a war footing whenever the word is uttered.

Each may have their own reasons to willfully distort what feminism is, yet the ultimate goal is the same. To maintain the institutional status quo. And just like anti-racism, this is precisely why we must take a view of feminism that does not focus merely on individual behavior, but one that focuses on power and systems.

Unfortunately, it's easier for many to wear the label of anti-racist than it is to wear the label of feminist. And, apparently, to those who feel this way, it's not even worth interrogating why.

We have to find a way past this, or at least get folks asking why they feel this way. Either sexism is a problem or it isn't. Acknowledging sexism is a problem but not feeling comfortable identifying with feminism is like saying that really bad B.O. is a problem and not feeling comfortable endorsing soap. On the other hand, claiming that sexism is not a problem and thus not feeling comfortable identifying with feminism is like saying that racism is not a problem but not being comfortable endorsing soap. (Think about it for a second.)

Feminism is a good thing, no matter how much sexism you think is left in the world. I remember a few years ago there was this meme with people explaining why "I don't need feminism" anymore. Which I personally think is absurd. But even if you believe that, sexism isn't some boss you beat at the end of a video game and you "don't need feminism anymore" because now you've got the cheat code. You always need feminism. Because the reality is that defeating sexism is more like killing Jason at the end of one of the Friday the 13th movies. You know there's gonna be a sequel.

Even if I killed the last zombie to end the zombie apocalypse, I'm probably still gonna carry my crossbow to the next few funerals I attend.

Now, before I use up all my pop culture analogies on this one issue, let me conclude with something I told that very reporter who asked that feminism gotcha question.

I said, "One of the first lessons I was taught about violence was that sticks and stones may break my bones but names can never hurt me. The moral being not to be afraid of what people say about you. Not to be cowed by someone using a word against you. Not to be beaten by someone calling you a name.

Yet it is my contention that we still have so many sticks and stones in this world because so many of us are afraid of being called one particular name.

We have to get past that. I'm not afraid of being called a feminist. I am a feminist. And I'm going to win a Republican primary and a U.S House Seat as one.

So thank you for the question."

Second Amendment Originalist

Excerpt from Interview on The Conversation, TYT

Something you haven't talked much about on the campaign trail is guns. What's your stance on the Second Amendment?

My stance on guns is that I don't have to have much of a stance at all. The stance is already there. If you told me I had to choose one part of the constitution to apply an originalist position in a case before the Supreme Court, it would be the Second Amendment. Anyone trying to dress up an interpretation of the Second Amendment in their own personal convenience shows contempt for James Madison, drafter of our beloved Bill of Rights.

And what about gun control?

I think you stop referring to it as gun control. People don't like the idea of someone else having control over them, and gun owners aren't any different.

If you wouldn't call it gun control, then what would you call it?

I'd call it gun safety. And because most of the gun owners I know believe in a myriad of safety measures, I would start crafting legislation by asking gun owners themselves.

A responsible gun owner doesn't want to see guns get into the wrong hands any more than someone who's anti-gun. But more than that, it's the vast knowledge of gun owners regarding the technical aspects of revolvers and various long guns that make them an asset in the conversation over sensible gun legislation.

After which, I'd probably defer to measures fought for by the NRA before they became intoxicated with money and power.

Back when NRA chief executive Franklin L. Orth proclaimed, "The NRA does not advocate an 'ostrich' attitude toward firearms legislation," because they recognized "that the dynamism and complexities of modern society create new problems which demand new solutions."

That's who the NRA was before they began putting their leaders' interests above the interests of the average gun owner. That's who the NRA was before they were taking in so much corporate cash they forgot what their original mission even was. That's who the NRA was before they became part of the DC swamp.

I'm willing to listen to good faith arguments on either side. What I'm not willing to entertain is corruption. Gun owners deserve better than corrupt advocates.

And what about those who don't own guns?

They deserve to be heard too. But I'm not sure the question itself is relevant. Because it implies that everyone who doesn't own a gun is anti-gun. And that is not the case.

So what about those who are anti-gun?

They deserve to be heard too. But I would make the same request of them that I would make of the staunchest of gun defenders. And that is to get educated on the other side of the issue, so when we *all* come to the table we can have a good faith discussion.

What about you? Are you pro-gun or anti-gun?

Well, that is a personal question. And I don't believe you make laws based on personal preferences. But I understand why you're asking, and I think it deserves an honest answer, as long as we both agree that honesty can be quite nuanced.

Now, I *personally* couldn't give a shit about guns. If there was a gun rapture tomorrow and all the guns just ascended into heaven, it wouldn't weigh any more on my mind than if there was a kombucha rapture.

But just like I'm not going to try and outlaw the abomination that is kombucha, I have no interest whatsoever in trying to outlaw guns.

And I'll let my voters in on a little secret. Neither do the Democrats.

The Democrats may be full of shit on a whole lot of plains, and they may be in complete opposition to my voters on certain policy issues, but we have to maintain some dignity in this conversation.

Ain't nobody coming for your guns. And ain't nobody coming for your guns because they know your ass wouldn't give them up if they did.

And what do you say to Republican voters who see no compromise with Democrats?

The compromise isn't with the Democratic Party. It's with our neighbors.

I'm doing my best to be honest in this campaign. But that means I expect a certain amount of honesty back. I do believe Democrats should listen, and I mean really listen, to responsible gun owners as it pertains to sensible gun legislation. But I also believe Republicans should listen, and I mean really listen, to those who've lost loved ones to accidental gun deaths, to suicide, to gun violence and mass gun violence and try their very best to imagine what compromises can be made to prevent situations like that from happening.

Both Democrat and Republican politicians have exploited this issue in different ways. Both have been disingenuous; both have been shortsighted. There are alternatives to the status quo of 30,000 gun deaths each year. Those numbers are not inevitable, as evidenced by our nearest gun loving neighbor Canada having a mere fraction of that. But to get those numbers to fall, we have to be able to have an honest conversation with good faith actors about all the elements that contribute to this national shame. A conversation free from grandstanding and free from industry greed.

I tell my voters, "I'm not here to echo everything you believe. Neither am I here to cheerlead industry talking points. I'm here to treat you like grownups. You deserve a voice in this conversation. All I want to do is make sure that conversation is a good faith one, on all sides."

Note:

I believe this conversation must be a diverse one. Not just bringing together a diversity of opinions over whether guns are good or bad, but diversity within the gun owning community at large. Meaning we have to hear from women. Women are half the population, and there's a whole lot of women who own guns. Secondly, I think we have to hear from non-Republican gun owners. Contrary to the political propaganda on this issue, there's a shitload of the population left of the political center who own guns, just as there are a whole lot of Republicans that don't own guns. Furthermore, we have to hear from minority gun owners, as well as gun owners who may have lost a loved one in either a suicide, accident, or gun crime.

This is not a black and white/wrong and right matter. It is nuanced, and there can be varying stances within the United States' broad gun-owning community. Like most issues, I see this as one that must be tackled holistically and institutionally. Our gun violence problem is indeed a violence problem. Just like our gun suicide problem is indeed a suicide problem. Sure, less guns would mean less gun deaths, but we're not getting rid of guns in the United States of America. It ain't happening. And even if it did, we'd still have a violence problem.

We should most definitely do everything we can to reduce the number of guns that can be accessed for either nefarious or desperate purposes. But we must also address the roads that lead to violence, the roads that lead to crime, and the epidemic absence of mental health.

Anyone who knows me knows that I have no love for guns whatsoever. But I think, while we may begin this conversation with emotion, we must in the end act on informed logic. And just like with the issue of abortion, we had to run our campaign not according to who we wished voters to be, but on where we wanted to go with them.

We're The Small In Small Government

Excerpt from Interview with Barry Stinson, WPHN Sinclair Broadcasting

Mr. Valentine, in your speech last week, you told the crowd at Aardvark's Fireworks that you should win this election by default. What did you mean by that?

I meant that there's zero reason to vote for my opponents in this race, because my opponents in this race don't believe in government. And I believe you should only run for things you believe in.

What do you mean they don't believe in government?

I mean that government boils down to two basic things: how we allocate common resources and how we balance freedoms. In other words, how we pay for shit and how we protect against shit.

In our current iteration of government, taxes pay for shit and regulations protect us against greed. Taxes pay for shit. Regulations protect us against greed.

And while there are varying opinions on civil liberties, which is a part of the balancing freedoms concept, the main discrepancy my opponents and I have over government is taxes and regulations.

And civil liberties aside, if you don't believe in the utility of taxes and regulations, then you don't believe in government.

I don't think your opponents would say they don't believe in government.

Oh, you don't believe me? That's ok. You don't have to take it from me. You can take it from them. They'll tell you. They don't favor taxes. They favor charity.

Ok. Then run for a fucking charity. But charity ain't government. Charity ain't paying for shit like roads and bridges and street lights, and schools and libraries and fire departments. Neither is it paying for law enforcement, a judicial system, or a military. Charity ain't paying for none of that.

Same thing with regulations. They'll straight up tell you. They don't favor regulations. They favor the market. And we vote for these people. You had Texans with a $10,000 heating bill who voted for politicians who can talk all day long about how "we don't need regulation; the market will just take care of people." Oh, it took care of 'em all right. Took *good* care of 'em.

It's not that difficult, man. Taxes pay for shit. Regulations protect us against greed. And if you don't agree with that, if you think charity should pay for shit and the market will protect us, then go run to be leaders in that world.

But I'm running for office in this world. A world where I believe we need a functioning and just government. I believe that. I believe in government. And you should only run for something if you believe in it.

It's the reason I didn't run for Vice-Sorcerer of Scientology when the seat became vacant. It might feel good to win, but I just don't believe I'd be an effective leader.

All jokes aside, Mr. Valentine, don't you think that's an exaggeration of their position on small government?

Actually, I don't. I think it's worse than what I just said. I don't think they care one way or the other about lower taxes or less regulations or any of that shit. I think their ideal government is really just a government with the least input from its citizenry. A government with the absolute smallest accountability to its voters.

That's what they mean when they say small government. They're talking about us. The small refers to our power. We're the small. So small, they can barely even see us. And because they can barely see us, they don't really have to pay attention to us.

So who are they paying attention to?

Who do you think? Corporations and rich people. That's the donors. And my opponents believe what the donors believe. And the donors believe if you pay for something, it's yours. That's why the donors run the show.

They believe it's their government, not ours. And my opponents believe the same thing.

There are a lot of people who are going to hear that and think it's an oversimplification.

Oh, I think it's simple. But not oversimple.

Whatever the powerful want, the politicians believe.

If the powerful wanted less mustard in their potato salad and less pimentos in their pimento cheese, small government would mean that.

Instead, corporations want less regulation. So my opponents' ideal government has less regulations. Rich people want less taxes, my opponents' ideal government has less taxes.

The average person on the other hand wants better wages, healthcare, and education. The average person wants clean and safe water, air, land, food, and transportation. But you know what those things take in our current system of government? Taxes and regulations.

But that ain't my opponents' idea of government. My opponents' idea of government is small government. And small government really means small democracy.

But what about civil liberties? Don't you agree on civil liberties?

If they believed it, yeah. But they don't.

The civil liberties pose is just window dressing. It's cosplay for the culture war. That's how they get the votes.

Sure, they might pander to the churches or throw us a couple drug decriminalization bones.

But you start talking about the civil liberty to organize and form a union for greater collective bargaining power, then all the sudden we're too small to see anymore.

You get what I'm saying? We're the small in small government.

So are you literally calling for your opponents to drop out of the race?

All I'm saying is if they wanted to be part of their ideal government, they would have run to be on the board of Lockheed Martin or Citibank. But instead, they're standing in the way of democracy.

But the polls show a lot of voters disagree with your assessment.

That's because every ataboy politician, every think tank lackey, every snake oil selling economist, and every business media boot licker has told them that small government is the way to go.

And forgive me for saying so, but reporters like you give my opponents cover instead of calling them out on their bullshit.

That's why the polls are the way they are. With as much propaganda as is thrown around, it's a minor miracle we ever elect anything but lukewarm empty suits.

I just think voters should know. My opponents are not really running for the office you're voting for.

If we're going to understand what we're voting for, we have to understand what office our politicians are really running for.

And if you want to vote for your Representative in the US House, I'm the only one really running for that position.

And what are your opponents running for?

You tell me. Who's the regional managers in this area? Who are the big corporations, the big money interests in this region? We can name 'em if you want. The point is that those are your regional managers. And the local managers, i.e., your district or state politicians, work under their supervision.

But, see, I'm not running to work for them. I'm running to work for the people. I'm running to be an assistant to the people - within the halls of Congress.

But my opponents? My opponents are running to be the assistant regional manager. Excuse me, assistant *to* the regional manager.

Ok, Mr. Valentine, I think we get the picture.

Office Reference!

Note:

In our current iteration of political/economic debate, the rich's advice to the poor is not to focus on exploding inequality and imploding democracy, but rather to focus on just how delectable you can make the crumbs flicked and the leftovers flung oh so charitably from their champagne stained tables. Think of it as soul food for the 21stCentury.

It's the reason why we have modern day philanthropy in the first place. It's legacy control for those who had the money and didn't really need it, at the same time when *you* needed the money and didn't really have it.

You deserve good healthcare, you deserve good schools, you deserve an earth worth your kids' future. You deserve more than being bullshitted. We live in the wealthiest country in the world, yet half of us are on the cusp of having nothing.

Our charities aren't a point of pride; they're a point of shame. The better a government functions, the less need there is for charities.

The sheer number of charities and nonprofits in this country, many of which were formed to pick up the pieces of slack-ass regulation, is all the proof you need for how our prevailing vision of government is a design of failure.

Still, the media allows this insulting debate to continue over small government vs. big government. I believe we deserve better than that shit. I believe we deserve a functional and just government. And I believed that voters believed that too. That's the reason why I ran. And it's the reason why I need more people to join me.

Redefine Policing

Excerpt from speech given at Handlin Auditorium

Although I agree we often get sidetracked with semantics, I do believe that words matter. That's why I don't use the slogans "defund the police" or "abolish the police." Not because I haven't read and listened enough to understand the demands, but because I know that too many people will hear either of those two slogans and will assume enough to not look into what they really mean. Moreover, I think these approaches may be too limited in scope.

That's why I prefer to use the slogan "Redefine Policing." If we can redefine policing in a manner that both narrows and improves the interactions we expect police officers to address, not just for us civilians but also for the men and women we expect to respond to such calls, policy implementation would be far less contentious.

In short, the goal of Redefine Policing is really just to make sure our police interactions don't suck, for anyone.

And one of the first ways we can ensure that is to eliminate all the situations that we currently send police to but don't really need to send police to. Police are not mental health professionals. Police are not medical professionals. Police are not required for parking violations, traffic accidents, welfare checks, missing persons, animal complaints, or the myriad of other calls we send armed officers out to address.

And it's not just about sending other people to do the work. I think we have to address why we send anybody out at all. Why in the fuck do police have to bother with what a free person wants to put into their body? End the drug war completely. Tax drugs like every other product we consume and treat addiction as what it is, a health issue. Furthermore, can we please take a look at what good it really does society to handle misdemeanor level offenses the way we do? Not only could we handle these violations in a way that doesn't disrupt or alter people's lives, we could quit wasting the time and energy of officers we need to handle far more serious issues.

Because, yes, even if we checked off every box on the "defund police" list, or hell even the "abolish police" list, you're still going to need highly trained and possibly well-armed men and women to answer calls concerning potential homicide, rape, aggravated assault, and robbery in progress. And whether you want to call them police or do away with the word altogether and make up a new word, we're still going to need someone to answer those calls.

Luckily, in the average precinct, violent crime makes up about 4 to 5 percent of 911 calls. Now, I'm not saying that's the only thing we would use our newly redefined police for, but I am saying that if we narrow the circumstances in which we expect to deploy such training, it would afford us adequate time and resources to maintain that training. Training that is ongoing and guided by the number one principle of De-escalation. Not to mention, it would afford us the resources to provide proper mental health and therapy for the PTSD these officers might acquire in the harshest of calls.

Because again, Redefine Policing is about protecting both civilians and the men and women we ask to fill these roles.

And yet, when I say Redefine Policing, it goes far beyond policing. We can't just treat this as a response to police brutality. If this is going to work, it has to be a response to society's brutality.

Part of the discussion over Redefine Policing has to be a discussion about the societal factors that contribute to the types of situations for which police officers get a call from dispatch. Many of said factors being political matters within our sphere of influence.

If you have an economy that leaves people economically vulnerable or desperate, an economy that then promotes an every man for himself mentality, you're going to see people act without regard for the interests of others.

If you have an educational system that leaves people without the critical thinking skills to make good decisions at the most critical times, you can expect them to fail themselves and the ones they love.

If you have a population without strong media literacy, they're going to be susceptible to the accumulation of negative images and messaging within certain news, entertainment, and social media.

If you have a private sector and a public sector that views mental health and/or addiction as a break within the villager and not the village, that village is going to break down.

If you have a society without community, a society that offers more opportunities for isolation than connection, you're going to have a society without the solidarity needed to survive with any sense of dignity.

Law enforcement can't be just a matter of insurance against the worst of our nature; it has to be an investment in the best of our nature.

But what are we investing in?

Don't we want a society with less 911 calls?

If so, then what are we investing in?

We have to be proactive in preventing 911 calls, rather than just preparing to be reactive to 911 calls.

Obviously, we want better law enforcement interactions. But this isn't just about that moment. It's about every moment that led up to that moment. And those moments are the yield of our societal investment. We get out what we put in. And anyone who doesn't believe that needs only observe the various models of societal investment around the world and the very different outcomes they yield.

However, until we can get to that place, we do have to focus on that moment of police interaction. A friend of mine who was a cop told me one time that he had to constantly remind himself that he only saw people when they were at their lowest moments.

Meaning, any other time, his perception of that person's potential would be completely different.

We don't need the people who respond to the lowest moments of our brothers and sisters to mirror them in that situation. We need someone who can bring them back from that lowest moment. Someone whose every motive is to de-escalate the situation and ensure no one gets hurt any more than they already are.

We need someone who will not isolate our brother or sister any more than they are already isolated in that moment, but rather to begin *in that moment* to build back the connection they've lost. We need someone who will do this, who will de-escalate at every turn, because they see that stranger as their own brother or sister.

I'm not claiming that's easy. I'm claiming the opposite. That's difficult. It's very difficult. But that's why the bulk of officer training has to be de-escalation. Of all the duties they're expected to perform, they must see their supreme role as de-escalation.

In fact, I would suggest as we redefine the role, we change the title to what it is we need in the role. I don't want to send police out to a volatile situation. I want to send de-escalators to that situation, just like the people who call 911 want to see people show up who can de-escalate the hell out of any situation.

If we already plan on narrowing the calls we have to send these men and women to, then why not transform their particular division of our societal response teams into an elite De-escalation Unit. Highly trained mitigators of potentially harmful situations. That's what we should want. Because what we should want is for everybody to be able to move forward from that situation with the absolute least harm done.

And for all those who feel like I'm avoiding or skating around the original issue that brought us to this place, let me dispel you of that notion. Part of this transformation, part of this new regiment of ongoing training, will be a theory and practice immersion into the psychological and sociological elements that shape our feelings, attitudes, and actions regarding race. A discernment informed by the context of A) historical oppression, B) our own implicit biases, and C) our varying degrees of institutional hierarchy.

We want to train and retrain and retrain the racism, if not fully out of the individual, at least out of their interactions with the public. And the same goes for sexism, classism, homophobia, and/or every other manifestation of macho bullshit.

And for anybody who thinks that cops won't go for that, I think you're wrong. And the ones who won't go for it are the ones we don't need anyway. Because as we narrow the size of these highly trained De-escalation Units, we can afford salaries that will have qualified and desirable candidates lining up around the block.

"Redefine Policing" is not just about how to better address mine or your lowest moments; it's about addressing those same places inside the ones sent out to help us.

And just as our response teams must be prepared to intercept an individual's descent before that descent goes too far, "Redefine Policing" must be about a nation of people who look out for each other and prepare each other so we may avoid falling in the first place.

Note:

We should always be striving to make our world a better world, and at times part of that may be to rethink and redefine what we thought we had figured out. As we redefine the role of policing, we have to focus on the de-escalation of so many different types of situations. And if we are thinking big picture, that concept of de-escalation must also apply to the societal circumstances and institutional momentum that lend to eventual 911 worthy situations.

Though without getting too holistic and missing the more immediate task at hand, we have to acknowledge that our goal of Redefine Policing is really about redefining police culture. And since, policy-wise, training may be the greatest influence we have to exert on these men and women, we have to first view the culture of this new De-escalation Unit through the lens of training.

And I don't mean some certificate of achievement you can throw in a desk or a closet and never have to think about again. I'm talking about the kind of training you would do in a jujitsu class, where you train, and train constantly, for every possible scenario. And in that training you rehearse your de-escalation moves, so before long those moves become a part of your muscle memory. And de-escalation becomes second nature. That's the type of culture we want.

But it's not just the moves; it's why you're doing the moves. Skills don't mean shit if the attitude and motivation isn't there to deploy them. Part of creating a culture of de-escalation is to maintain the gravity of why a 911 call has been placed. That somewhere somehow something has broken down, and you are there to make sure it doesn't break down any further. For a society, it is a role that is both regrettable and hopeful. Regrettable that our community was not able to catch our brother, our sister, before they fell. Hopeful that we can still be there to help them get back up.

In addition to training, there's different incentive and reward structures that can be put in place to help along this reshaping of culture. And when we're deciding upon which structures to employ, we have to look around at what has been tried and what has been successful. We have to be evidence-based and committed to the most desirable outcome.

This, of course, doesn't mean we won't experiment. It means that our experiments have to be both efficiency and justice minded. If we're going to arm our De-escalation Units with devices designed to potentially subdue someone, we need to think in the same terms that doctors think. First, do no harm. And I don't care if that means using a goddamn human sized butterfly net; we have to foresee and design these situations with the best end result in mind. And the best end result is the least harm done.

It ain't always gonna be that easy. But it's achievable. And there are entire countries that have proven they can go 365 days of emergency calls and not have their police kill one person.

It's not just on the person being called out to an emergency location. It's on the training and the culture *we give* the one we trust to de-escalate the situation.

But more than that, it's on the environmental, economic, and societal scenario we place our neighbors, our loved ones, our brothers and sisters in. We can make the misuse of drugs the justification for help and care. We don't have to make the use of drugs the justification for war. We can treat the absence of mental health as an opportunity to reestablish connection. We don't have to treat it as an opportunity to police people in crisis. We can teach our children empathy and critical thinking skills, not just in our homes, but in our schools, every year their brains continue to develop. Or we can roll the dice on whatever else is being shoveled into their brains.

Each non-accident 911 call is a failing, not just of an individual, but of society. If we expect men and women to sign on to become de-escalators, it's our responsibility as a society to try and minimize the amount of calls they will have to answer. We can't be reactive. We have to be proactive. And that means redefining a whole lot more than just policing.

Ain't Nothing Wrong With Our Children

Excerpt from the NNPA Parents Forum address at Davey Ballpark

Shouldn't our education system be aspirational for the kind of life we want for our children? Shouldn't we model our schools on the kind of adults we want them to become and the kind of society we want them to live in?

I don't think it's controversial to assume that most people would answer yes to that.

And yet the overwhelming majority of our schools are still based on the assembly line model of education.

If we want a better world, we have to build that better world. And building a better world starts with education. In a better world, we would employ technological innovation to make obsolete the rote and soul killing assembly line jobs that no one dreams about having when they're a child. Likewise, we must use whatever resources are at our disposal to make obsolete the rote and soul killing assembly line model of schooling.

There are alternatives. There are other ways to teach our children. And these alternatives are not theoretical. They're tested. They're proven. In other countries and in the communities that have tried them in this one.

What they are not is the status quo. Meaning it's going to take a whole lot of educators and a whole lot of parents taking a chance on change. But that chance is only asking, "Can our children do as well as those other children? Do our children have the same capacity for learning as children in the best educated countries?"

I believe they do. Ain't nothing wrong with our children. Something wrong with us. In that we are too reluctant to take that chance on change. We are too reluctant to take that chance for our children.

And what's the main reason we are so reluctant? Because that kind of change, at least in the beginning, would cost a good deal of money. As if we've got anything better to spend our tax dollars on. Because, remember, if we screw this up, it's all screwed up.

We have to pay for what's important. Is anything more important than this?

Yes, this change would require an investment. The problem is, when it comes to our precious taxes, too many of us focus on the price tag, rather than the return on that investment.

When it comes to education, we shouldn't be thinking in terms of "whatever we can get away with." We should be thinking in terms of "whatever it takes." Because in the final analysis, "whatever it takes" is going to be the right investment.

I know we got a lot of "can't get right"s in this society. Grown folks who should know better. Grown folks out there fucking it up for the rest of us.

But I also know that a whole lot of those people were failed by a whole lot of us.

I think of education like Reverse Engineering. In that we should think first about the kinds of adults that make our world a great place to live in. And I'm not just talking about the kind of adults who can contribute productive labor. I'm talking about the kind of adults who can appreciate all that life and humanity have to offer, who are generous, respectful and empathetic, who can critically think and not let their emotions get the best of them. Family, friends, and neighbors you can depend on to not fuck it up for the rest of us.

We have to think about the qualities that go into these kinds of adults, the principles that build their foundation. And then we have to build that foundation. We have to reverse engineer our children's education based on our best possible selves. Just like we should be reverse engineering our society based on the value lessons we teach our children. Lessons like "don't lie, don't cheat, don't steal. It's not if you win or lose, but how you play the game."

Can any of us look around at the way we've structured our government, our economy, our social relations, and think we're living up to those lessons?

It's no wonder so many of our children grow up not adhering to those lessons. It's because everything around them, including far too often their own parents, are telling them with their actions, "That's just something you say, not something you do."

It's not enough to just change the elementaries, the middle schools, the high schools, the colleges. We have to change all the other schools our children are taught in. From the home to the workplace to the pews to the stands to the screens to the pages to the polling stations to the streets, we adults have to view ourselves as both students and educators. And we have to take inventory on the lessons we take in and the lessons we teach on a daily basis.

Schools ain't gonna do it all. But if we can be cognizant of the other schools we learn from and contribute to, we might have a shot at building that necessary foundation. Not just for better students, but for a better world.

In the meantime, though, we have to focus on what we have the most control over right now. This is about the elementaries, the middle schools, the high schools, and so on.

Let's look at what has worked in other places. Let's look at what else they do to make it work. Let's think about the outcome we want, and let's do whatever it takes to make that change.

Or else, we're the ones that are fucking it up for the rest of *them*.

Note:

When we talk about education, we're primarily talking about two things. The method and the money.

As it pertains to the method, I think there's multiple directions we can go. That is, as long as we agree that we *have* to run the fuck away from the assembly line model of schooling.

Just like our economic model, just like our model of governance, too many of us act like what we've been doing in education, since before most homes had a television, has to be the way we do it 'til the end of time.

It's like when I hear people say, "That's the way I was raised, and I turned out ok." No, you didn't. You didn't. And you know how I know? Because you're running around saying dumbass shit like that.

That's only slightly different than hearing people excuse away not having a real argument by saying, "Well, I'm sorry, but that's just the way I was raised." That's not an answer. That's an admission that you don't really know why you believe what you believe. Which makes sense because most of our assembly line education is based on memorization that goes in one ear and leaves out your ass once the big test is over.

We can't continue to ignore that there are other ways to do things. And when it comes to education, there's a whole lot of other ways. From the Deweyite schools to the Montessori model to the Waldorfs and the Sudburys to the Krishnamurti schools, we have to start looking at what produces the most well-rounded critical thinkers.

Yet in order to do that, it requires that *we* do some critical thinking.

When challenged about my (lefty) intentions at a voter forum on education, I didn't bullshit the audience. And I didn't back down. I just paused, looked around the room, and told them, "Sure, we want children who are less prone to settling disputes with violence when they grow up. But if I tell you about the Empathy curriculum in Danish schools, all of the sudden that's some liberal feminist shit. Pussifying our boys and turning them into pansies.

Sure, we want our children to grow up and be able to decipher fake news from real news. But the moment you introduce media literacy, philosophy, or logic classes? Well, now, you're indoctrinating our children.

Sure, we want an education that is the absolute best for our child. But when we hear about this experiential learning and flexibly structured, student-centered curriculum, it triggers thoughts of entitlement and participation trophies. And don't even talk about no homework or no grades. That'll just produce a generation of softserve weaklings.

Except it doesn't. We have to make these decisions based on evidence. And what the evidence bears out is sometimes hard for us to take. Especially when we see that our lives might have been vastly different had *our* schooling been so vastly different.

Education isn't about beating information into children as they move down the conveyor belt. It's about giving them the right tools to figure out how to make their own moves."

Of course, that was just about the method. We haven't even got to the money part.

And what really is there to say about the money part other than you get what you pay for? We've got crumbling roads and bridges because we won't properly invest in infrastructure. We've got lead in our water because we didn't want to change the pipes. We've got a planet that is racing toward being uninhabitable because we don't want to be honest about the fundamentals of our economy.

All of the remedies are within our reach. But we're not going to achieve any of it if we don't produce concerned, informed, civically engaged citizens. And we're not going to produce those kinds of adults unless we pay for the education our children deserve.

It's the method and the money. We can change the way we handle both. But only if we're willing to address the issue with more than just "That's the way I was raised, and I turned out ok."

Free Speech Country

Excerpt from speech at the Chafin Road VFW

I'll be the first to admit that, when it comes to the issue of speech, the Left has a self-righteous problem. Far too many of us act as if we came out the womb quoting Marx and Simone de Beauvoir.

But worse than that, we sometimes act offended and/or attacked when someone is not as far along in the journey as we believe that we are. And that is a huge turn off to the people we should be trying to attract to our side. But rather than doing the hard work of organizing more and more of those folks into our movement, we opt for the immediate gratification of shaming all those who do not follow the most recent edition of the "how to be a good leftist" manual, the most recent edition having been written by that particular self-righteous leftist.

Y'all know what I'm talking about. I can't stand that shit. It's like a mechanic screaming at me and calling me a bastard because I don't know exactly how a transmission works. Yes, I should probably know. But that doesn't mean I'm a piece of shit because I forget what torque was.

With that said, if I insist that the transmission is responsible for shooting out the wiper fluid and then cite the First Amendment when you point out how wrong I am, that's not cool either.

To which, I am referring to my friends on the other side of the ideological aisle. If the Left has a self-righteous problem, the Right has an opinion problem.

Too many of my friends on the right believe they live in Free Speech Country, when they really live in Opinion Land. Free Speech Country is about free speech. Opinion Land is about *my* speech. In Free Speech Country, the First Amendment guarantees your right to voice your opinion. In Opinion Land, the First Amendment guarantees that your opinion is all that matters.

But you can't run a civilization on opinion.

A civilization needs things like science and empirical data. Verifiable shit.

Unfortunately, in some provinces of Opinion Land, any of that verifiable shit that conflicts with your opinion is automatically dismissed as fake news.

So what the hell do we do? One of the reasons why we have so much animosity in our politics is that the worst of the Left are often the most vocal, and the worst of the Right are often the most vocal. Not coincidentally, most of that worstness is vocalized online.

Which, if we really want to begin dismantling some of that worstness, we have to quit living so much of our lives online. Log off, walk outside, talk to your neighbors, talk to people who don't look like you, who don't think like you. Talk to folks who you might normally be suspicious of their politics. Chances are, you'll find out they're not all that bad. You may vehemently disagree on matters of policy, but what are the areas of common ground you share? What are the shared needs, the shared dreams, you have for your family and your loved ones?

For it is that shared common ground that we have to start at. It is that shared common ground that we must use as a foundation, if we are to build any semblance of discourse and political dialogue.

You can have all the free speech in the world. It won't mean shit if we see each other as enemies. It won't mean shit if we live in different realities. If free speech is to mean anything, it takes more than just speech. It takes listening. Real listening.

The kind of listening that keeps us *wanting* to be honest actors. The kind of listening that leads us to debate in good faith and argue based on evidence.

The issue then is: what does good faith mean? For that matter, what does evidence mean? We have to acknowledge there are certain standards we should demand from our information sources, from our news sources, just as there are certain ground rules we should establish for debate.

However, as much as I would like to live in a world where such standards were the highest concern, free speech doesn't guarantee honest actors. And there will always be parties who are not interested in truth or accountability. And those parties will, as sure as the day is long, cite the First Amendment as their excuse as to why they don't feel the need to be held to any kind of standards or mutual trust.

And ultimately, they'll be right. Because free speech does not require anyone to abide by these standards. It does not require you to be factual or logical or ethical.

That's why free speech requires those on the *receiving* end of their information to be prepared.

If you're a parent, you can't monitor all the garbage entertainment your kids are being bombarded with, just like you can't stop all the actual fake news being thrown at your friends and family. We don't want the wrong lessons to be learned any more than we want wrong information to guide our decision making.

But because we *do* believe in free speech, the only real comfort you can take is when you know your children, your family, your friends are prepared. That is precisely why we must begin offering classes that build a foundation of critical thinking skills and media literacy in our population. If we are to produce well-informed, highly discerning, civically engaged citizens, these classes are every bit as important as reading, math, and science.

And I'm not just talking about K-12 either. I would encourage participation in these types of classes throughout the entirety of our time on this earth. From the community colleges to the nursing homes, I would make such classes free, and I would even go as far as to offer economic incentive for folks to attend. Think of it as a booster shot for democracy. Where the return on investment far outweighs the cost up front.

And don't just take it from me; take it from gun owners. Every gun owner I know, every believer in the Second Amendment, will tell you they're wholeheartedly in favor of responsible gun ownership, which means learning and relearning about precaution, best practices, and safety measures. Many gun owners will periodically take refresher courses in these areas, because they take seriously the responsibility that goes along with their freedom.

All freedoms come with responsibility. If we are to embrace free speech, if we are to embrace the First Amendment the same way we expect gun owners to embrace the Second Amendment, we must embrace the responsibility that comes along with that freedom.

And you know how you can tell when you've embraced that responsibility? You know how you can tell when someone is responsible enough to safely handle free speech? When we're able to ask questions that would normally be too uncomfortable for us to ask and when we're ok with admitting we could be wrong.

We can't live in Opinion Land. And we can't be self-righteous know-it-all assholes. We have to be able to ask questions, admit when we're wrong, and see each other as worth doing the hard work that that takes.

Note:

As I said in my address, free speech doesn't guarantee honest actors. And if we are to get to a place where we can trust our information sources, it's going to take a cooperation that we're not used to seeing.

I personally think a good start would be to invite all interested parties to come together and agree upon a sniff test for bullshit. And I'm talking everyone. From Fox News to MSNBC, from the New York Times to the Washington Times, from the Wall Street Journal to the Intercept, from establishment journalists to indie journalists. All parties who are interested, all parties who answer this invitation, would have a chance not only to help create a litmus test to ensure the integrity of rival news organizations, but a litmus test to vouch for their own.

Think of it like a checklist that can be monitored by all, in accordance with such agreed upon guidelines. A transparent system that can be pointed to if any one member within this consortium of accountability strays from what is verifiable. Where agreeing to be part of this consortium, and to be held by such standards, affords that journalist or journalistic operation a certain amount of public trust.

The same goes for methods of argumentation. Far far far too often, our pundits and pontificators spew all manner of horse manure in the gamble that those listening won't be skilled enough in the ways of deceit to recognize the smell. In which case, we need a sort of anti-checklist. Where if any of the boxes on that list get ticked off, it calls into question the information and/or motivation of said actor.

Now, I'm not claiming to have all the answers. Nor am I smart enough to tell you what a list of fair standards would even look like. I can imagine the journalism schools and the News Guild and the news watchdogs might have far better suggestions for reporting accountability. Just as there is all manner of already agreed upon criteria to spot intellectually dishonest arguments and debate tactics that could be monitored by independent experts.

I'm just saying we must extend the invitation. Because if it could mean more people being able to rightly trust their news, more people being able to rightly trust the voices within political and economic and social discourse, I think it would be well worth (and I would be willing to introduce legislation) funding such an accountability consortium, if and only if it was non-partisan and its membership was voluntary.

Which brings us to those who would not answer that invitation, those parties who are not interested in mutual trust or accountability. It's not just about how to get the honest actors to work together. It's about protecting ourselves against the dishonest actors. And, regardless of one's circumstances, the only real defense we can reliably mount against the weaponization of speech is a strong mind.

But strong minds are not a given.

The same people who think the market will just sort everything out in a fair and equitable manner are the same people who pretend that you can just set free speech loose without any societal responsibility to provide the population with historical and social reference, critical thinking skills, and media literacy.

You can't be a free speech absolutist unless you immediately follow up such proclamation with how you plan to develop and nurture the kinds of minds that can detect and discern and decide with some baseline competence.

Anyone who's ever worked in advertising, public relations, entertainment, or the news *knows* that speech is not just an individual practice. It is a system. And if we are to have any chance against the not-so-benevolent actors within such industries, *we* must also look at speech as a system. Where the widespread belief in baseless conspiracy theories is seen as a failure of that system. Where the questions we find ourselves unable or unwilling to ask are evidence of the failure of that system. Where the ease of hoodwinking whole segments of society and the routine persuasion of voters to cast a ballot against their own interests must be viewed as a failure of our speech system.

Free speech isn't just about protecting the speech itself; it's about protecting the one who speaks it. But it should also be about protecting the one who will receive it and/or respond to it. By preparing folks to be responsible actors within an environment of free speech, we make our system of speech a healthy and just system.

But the way it is right now, critical thinking and critical questions are too often seen as attacks. Meaning, the expectation, in our current free speech system, is that we will merely consume whatever is produced. To be good consumers, but not good citizens. All just more evidence of the failure of this system.

On the contrary, in a healthy and just system of speech, institutions worthy of power, in order to keep themselves honest and *keep* themselves worthy of power, demand this type of critical thinking, demand this type of unflinching questioning.

In a healthy and just system, the most vocal experts and thought leaders would be those with humility and an understanding of how much there still is left to know.

But in our system, we find ourselves constantly embarrassed by two different kinds of know-it-alls.

On one side you have those who live in a constant state of online war over a reality of constantly evolving concepts and language that you damn near need a PhD to keep up with. On the other side, you have those in a constant state of online war where there is no reality outside of their own opinion or the opinion of the Dear Leader.

And I know I covered all this in my speech, but it's important enough to say again; it's important we see what we have to get past.

You've got people out there who vote on life and death issues, who impact not just their own future *but your future*, hollering, "Well, that's just my opinion." Well, goddamn it, that ain't good enough. You know what kind of motherfuckers say, "well, that's just my opinion"? Wrong motherfuckers.

When it's daytime, you can't just say it's your opinion that it's nighttime. That's not how opinions work. Your opinions still have to be based on something. The idea that opinions are just whatever you think is like - your opinion, man. Our minds should be flexible enough that, when faced with evidence that contradicts our opinions, they can be changed.

Yet when the facts don't support their arguments, these fools claim their opinion is being censored. But that's not how censorship works either. If society is not allowing you to literally say your opinions out loud, that is most definitely censorship. But to merely deny opinions being presented as facts, and/or to point out how fucking stupid your opinion is, is not censorship.

And rather than come to terms with such reasoning, a select few choose to flaunt their lack of reasoning under the guise of free speech. To them, the first amendment is really about the power to lack reasoning. And while I can't technically dispute that, I can point out that it's kind of like flaunting your premature ejaculation under the guise of free love.

Which brings me to my friends on the left who are lining up to cancel me for my unfair shaming of premature ejaculation and not being sex positive enough with my analogies.

As much as I shit on those living in Opinion Land for acting like the existence of people who disagree with them is an attack on their own existence, they're not the only ones playing that game. We can't tell the Right how dangerously close to authoritarian thinking it is for them to suggest their opinion is the only one that may be voiced when we treat *our own* speech as a bludgeon against anyone we spot with a wrinkle in their philosophical attire.

We have to be calling these people in, not calling these people out. You may not like doing it, but it's about more than what you like. If we want to win a better world, it can't be a world of conquest. It must be one in which we arrive there together. And that means movement building. And it means building a solidarity that is attractive and not merely respected out of fear.

And while all of this free speech stuff may seem like a strange thing to explicitly address during a campaign, I believed it was a necessary strategy. Because if voters simply retreated to Opinion Land, I was going to lose. By talking openly and candidly about this kind of stuff, my hope was that I'd be able to bring people's consciousness level to a point where they'd catch themselves before any such retreat occurred.

But more than that, I knew going in that many voters would disagree with me on a ton of issues, at least initially. And while it was vital that I called out corruption and venality within the system, calling out voters, the way too many on the left often viciously do, was not going to be a winning electoral strategy. That doesn't mean I couldn't engage in real talk. It just means I used that real talk to call voters in. I used that real talk to show voters I respected their intellect and sense of humanity in a way that my opponents did not. That I expected more from them than being duped by the corrupt and the venal.

Because if I couldn't respect GOP voters for their intellect and sense of humanity, if I couldn't expect more from them than what run of the mill Republican politicians expect from them, then there was no point in running. The only way we can ever truly listen to those on the other side of the political or ideological spectrum, which is what this campaign at its core was about, is to see them as more than opposition, as more than rivals, as more than a lost cause.

Excerpt from Interview with PBS reporter Sumita Chowdry

Mr. Valentine, in addition to getting money out of politics, you've touted your support for Ranked Choice Voting, or what used to be known as Instant Runoff Voting. Can you explain why you think this is so important?

I support this method of voting because I support expanding our democratic process. The more democracy the better.

And I support it because it's what the people want.

But polls show most voters aren't even aware of what Ranked Choice Voting is.

I didn't say they know what it is. I said it's what they want.

How can they want something they don't know about?

Because they want third parties. You go ask the first person, the first ten persons, the first one hundred persons, you meet on the street: If you could vote for a third party and *know* that they would have a shot at winning and *also know* that your vote would not result in the side you hate winning, would you do it? I guarantee you that 9 out of 10 voters would give you the biggest "hell yes" since Bill Clinton discovered anonymous chat rooms.

And you believe Ranked Choice Voting would provide the surety needed to vote for a third party candidate.

Not only do I believe *that*, I believe it would give incentive for voters to become more politically interested and active. As it stands right now, most of us vote against the candidate we hate, rather than for the candidate we love. In other words, in our current system most voters don't have to know shit, outside of who they think is full of shit.

And, you know, it's hard to argue with that mentality knowing how many Democrats don't really want democracy, and how many Republicans don't really like competition.

So how do you propose to get the public support needed to get something like this passed?

First, we gotta acknowledge that the main obstacle for Ranked Choice Voting is the very reason they quit calling it Instant Runoff Voting. It's a terrible fucking name. Whoever thought that Ranked Choice Voting was a better name deserves to get a wedgie by their own grandmother.

Then what would you call it?

Well, we've been crowd-sourcing different ideas for the last couple months, but ultimately it's not for me to decide. It's for the people who want third parties to decide. That's why I'm hosting a poll on my website that allows the people to choose what we should call it in my bill. And as you can probably guess, the poll is a ranked choice poll.

I'm personally going to vote for calling it Even Playing Field Voting. But we'll see what gets the most votes.

The point is we want to demonstrate how the system would work and why it's important. No one should have to dread doing their civic duty. And no one should have to worry that voting their conscience is going to screw over the country.

I assume that's why you're calling the bill the Vote No Evil Act?

That's right. For all the people who are tired of voting for the lesser of two evils, the Vote No Evil Act gives each and every one of these disaffected souls a reason to feel hopeful come time to cast their ballot.

And you don't think the name of the bill is going to be taken as an insult in the Congress?

Hell, they ought to be glad we went with that name. We were originally going to call it The Third Party Legalization Act.

But that. That right there. How do you expect something like this to garner enough votes to pass, if, by your own acknowledgement, it's not in the incumbents' interests to vote for it?

Because we're going to make it a Lose/Maybe Win situation.

What does that mean? Lose Maybe Win?

You've heard of a Win Win situation, and a Lose Lose situation. But this is a Lose/Maybe Win situation.

And I'll start with the Maybe Win part first. My message to the politicians I expect to vote yes on this bill is a challenge. Do you or do you not represent what the majority of your constituents want to see in their Congressional representative? Because right now, we don't know that. As long as there's no viable third parties, all most of these candidates do is just run against the other party. But if the field is open to multiple parties, who all have the same shot, then you have a real competition on your hands. And the only way these politicians can prove that they actually represent the majority's wishes is to pass this legislation and then run and win again. You do that, and I'll call you a winner. But until then, you ain't really won nothing. You're just less shitty than the only other choice people had.

Having said that, I think *there are* people who can do that, who can win in an open playing field. And that's the Maybe Win part.

So what about the Lose part?

The Lose part of the Lose/Maybe Win situation is the threat we have to coax out of the voters. We have to get the mass of voters all over this country, Democrat, Republican, and Independent, to contact their representatives, both House and Senate, and let them know of the pledge that they've made. And that pledge is a commitment to vote for anyone else but that individual in the next primary, unless these respective representatives vote yes on the Vote No Evil Act. Unless they can make future electoral contests open and truly competitive, they no longer deserve the seat they occupy. Democrat or Republican, they all have to go.

And for those we're asking to pledge, you don't even have to think about it as voting against that individual. You're voting against a rigged system. Because if they won't vote for this bill, it's because they prefer a rigged system. They're telling you that with their vote. And the only way we're going to get rid of this rigged system is to vote it out.

So if your weak ass wants to vote against this bill because you won't take the chance to run in an open and unrigged process, then you gotta lose automatically.

You can either defeat this bill and lose the next primary by default, or you can pass this legislation and maybe win in a fair fight. That's your choices. Either we're gonna get this legislation this time around with you. Or we're gonna get this legislation next time without you.

And you think you can get voters to pledge to that?

Hell yeah, I think I can. Voters want more competition in our elections. They love the idea of a third party candidate coming in and handing a politician their ass. And for those who do actually love their elected representative, or even love their party, this pledge doesn't require you do anything special in the general election. You can love on your party all you want in the general. We're just asking for *new* blood in your party, if the old blood isn't willing to trust you.

Because that's what rigged systems really say to voters anyway. That the establishment doesn't trust the voters. And any politician that doesn't trust you, you sure as hell shouldn't trust them.

Make them earn your trust. Make them show you their hand. Because, remember, hadn't none of them really earned the seat they're sitting in if they won that seat in an election that shut out third parties.

One last thing. You're running as a Republican. Doesn't opening the contest up to third parties actually threaten your chance of getting reelected if you could actually get this to pass?

Maybe. But that's ok too. Because even I won't have earned my seat until I've won it in an open contest. And if I lose that contest, that's ok too. Because, see, I'm not running to hoard power; I'm running to give it back. And if we can get money out of politics and/or make these elections real contests, then I'll welcome whatever comes after that.

Note:

If we are unable to get money completely out of politics, ranked choice voting, or as I refer to it "Open Playing Field Voting," may be the next best thing for ensuring that uncorrupt candidates have at least some shot at winning. Having the parties decide for you who is viable and who is not is simply not an option for a people who expect democracy.

Which is another reason why we have to forever put to bed the practice of partisan gerrymandering. The fact that this was ever commonplace in our politics, on either side, should be a cause of great shame.

If the parties truly believe in what many have called "a free market of ideas," then we must make sure that all ideas have an equal chance at being heard, and that the end contest is not skewed toward a particular candidate or candidates. I've suggested other policy mechanisms that would contribute to this goal, including national standards for easy voting and registration, independent debate boards, national holiday for elections, fair matching funds, and reasonable candidate access to all publicly owned airwaves or communications commons. And I believe all those are important. But outside the primary goal of getting money out of politics, I saw Open Playing Field Voting and third party liberation as a rallying cry that voters could get behind and see the benefits of, especially during their primaries.

Could I Really Vote For That Asshole

Excerpt from address at the Starcourt Theater

So it's getting close, y'all. Voting starts next week, and I know there are a lot of people in my district who have not made up their minds yet. No matter what the polls say right now, I know there are a whole lot of folks who are thinking to themselves, "Could I really vote for that asshole?"

And you know why they're asking themselves that? Because they want to vote for this asshole.

I was at a truck stop the other day, and I had a trucker come up to me. He told me he was going to vote for me, even though he disagreed with me on almost every issue. And after I said thank you, I asked him why. And he said that he was coming up on sixty, and he's never in his life had a chance to vote for an honest man.

That made me feel good. Made me feel like I'd made the right decision in running.

Then, not two minutes after he said that, I had another voter come up to me, a woman who worked at the truck stop, who told me she *couldn't* vote for me because she disagreed with me on almost every issue.

And that did not make me feel good. Made me *question* if I'd made the right decision in running. But rather than write her off, I asked her if she wouldn't mind listing for me the policies on which we didn't see eye to eye. And as she went down the list, I told her the same thing after each item. That she should vote for me. Over and over she would tell me a policy she disagreed with, and I would tell her that she should vote for me. And by the end, we were both laughing.

She said, "I could go on, but I know what you're going to say." And I said, "But do you know why I'm saying it?"

I told her that, if she wouldn't mind indulging me for just a little more, I'd like her to share with me the issues that were pressing in her life, the things that she really needed fixing in Congress. And after she gave me that list, I asked her if the politicians she was used to voting for over the last 20 years agreed with her on policy. She said yes. Then I asked her if any of those issues had been seriously addressed by the same politicians over the last 20 years. She said no.

I said that's why you should vote for me. You may not agree with how I think we could get there. But, for the issues you raised, the areas in your life that matter the most, we most definitely agree on where we need to get.

I told her I wasn't going to change my policy positions. But that I could do something for her that no politician she'd ever voted for had done. I told her that I could represent her, that I could do my best to make her situation better. I told her that the reason why nothing had gotten better for her over the last 20 years is because those politicians hadn't been representing her; they'd been representing the donors. They weren't doing their best for her; they were doing their best for the donors.

I've said a thousand times over this campaign, "Let's get money out of politics and see what happens." After that, it won't be about whether I was right or wrong. It will be about you.

Until we get money out of politics, it ain't about you. At least not with those other politicians.

Whatever our differences, I've never lied to you. I know that I'm asking you to take a chance. Maybe not as big a chance as me running in a Republican primary, but a chance nonetheless.

Take that chance. Let me represent your interests. Let me kick the donors in the balls.

It's your vote. Not theirs. Do something with it. Send a message to DC that shit is about to change. If I do nothing else in Congress, I will raise the bar on accountability, and I will raise hell doing it.

And if that's not worth taking a chance on, then I don't know what is.

Note:

Those last few weeks, it really started to set in. I had been focused so much on Election Day that I hadn't been thinking as much about the day after.

My original plan, in case I didn't win, was to present a kind of "shadow term" where I contrasted, on a weekly basis, what I would have done differently from what the winner of my primary actually did. Simultaneously, I would lend my newly acquired celebrity to left organizing and activism throughout the district and the state. The hopes were that I could continue to make folks of all political stripe less suspicious of left-minded entities, and my Shadow Term would keep my profile in the news to a degree that if I decided to run next go round, I'd have an even better chance at winning (especially considering that my opponent wasn't about to do shit with their term).

What I hadn't focused on, as much as I really should have, was the most important question of the campaign: What if I win? It's one thing to make the pros as an amateur. It's a whole other to play on a team you just spent the entire tryouts badmouthing the team captain.

Lucky for me, I didn't give a shit what the team owners thought. I was playing for the folks in the stands. And though I've certainly had my fair share of fumbles, what I believe I've proven, in the short amount of time I've served, is that your efficacy depends on your creativity. And that if you can get the people behind you, there's a path to change.

I've said it many times in these pages, and I'm going to say it again. I need help. I need more fighters in here with me. I did this with authenticity and audaciousness. We add numbers to that, and we're going to be unstoppable.

You can do this. We can do this. Let's show the people what democratic representation really looks like. And let's show the party bosses the goddamn door.

Epilogue: Guerilla Campaigning 101

Before the small dollar donations started rolling in, we didn't have, as my granny used to say, a pot to piss in or a window to throw it out. That was the same time I was getting schooled on just how much knowledge and work and coordination it took to run a campaign. Fortunately, we had some folks reach out to us who had previously worked on a couple epic upset primary victories in the Democratic Party who liked what we were doing and were generous enough to share their insight on insurgency campaigning.

Having those legal/logistics nuts and bolts laid out for us allowed our team to focus on our greater strategy with a confidence I know we wouldn't have had otherwise. For that, we will forever be grateful and have pledged to do the same for any GOP primary candidate willing to follow in my lefty spoiler footsteps.

Without, however, getting into all such behind-the-scenes minutiae, there are certain suggestions I would like to offer in these last pages. While I believe it is crucial to have a clear eye on the issues, with solid articulation of policy justification and benefits, let's not kid ourselves. This is a, let's call it, specific type of campaign. And it takes a specific type of candidate.

Obviously, there are certain intangibles that can't hurt. If you're good looking, great. If you have charm and charisma, great. If you have a quick wit and sharp sense of humor, great.

But, from my experience, what matters most is if people can relate to you. You can't be a fucking politician. You have to be a real person. Don't hide your quirks; make them work for you. Don't follow the playbook; follow your instincts. Relax and be yourself. If people see you as authentic, that automatically separates you from the vast majority of vote wranglers.

With that said, if your authentic self is not comfortable being absolutely audacious, then don't fucking bother. When the little guy takes on the big guy, his only chance is taking a chance. You have to be bold. You have to be willing to do what no one has done. And you have to be committed to the fight.

Any politician will tell you, the intangibles go a long way. Any voter will tell you, authenticity goes a long way. I'm telling you, if you're not a fighter, don't fucking bother.

Speaking of being a fighter, if you don't have bloody knuckles by the end of the first day, you're not doing it right. Not that I went out and beat my primary opponents to a pulp, but that I knocked on doors until I couldn't raise either arm.

When they say meet people where they are, I took that shit literally. Way I figured it, the best way to win a person is to be in person. You have to knock on doors. You have to show up. You have to go to where the people are. Let them see you, let them meet you, let them try you.

From the pool halls to the shopping malls, from the diners to the dinner table, be prepared to wear out your shoes, but know better than to wear out your welcome.

In addition to the discipline, determination, and stamina this type of fight demands, it also requires a pretty darn thick skin. A lot of folks aren't going to be feeling you. But they are going to make sure you feel them.

I must have been called every low-down bastard under the sun, with a few names I hadn't even heard before. And you know what I did after every "fuck you" yelled in my face? I looked that asshole straight in their bad breath and told them, "Message received, my friend. But I'm still determined to earn your vote."

And that wasn't a lie. I didn't take anyone for granted. Our ground game was goddamn legendary. Unless you were off the grid, you were on our radar. With a team of seasoned organizers behind me, we turned what was initially seen as the candidacy of an ideological carpetbagger into a handshaking, name taking, norm breaking, believer making, word of mouth miracle.

Unfortunately, you're never going to be able to meet everyone in the flesh. But what you can do is meet them on the screen. Meaning, if you don't have enough money to have your content run over and over across the airwaves (which your grassroots ass obviously won't), your only shot is putting out a shit ton of content on social media. And when I say a shit ton, I mean a shit ton. Content content content. If you're not ringing doorbells or shaking a bowling alley worth of hands, your ass better be making some content.

If you've got a policy, make a video repping that policy and post the hell out of it. If you give a speech, give it like you're leading an army into battle and post the hell out of it. If you do an interview, blow that interviewer's goddamn mind... and post the hell out of it.

Furthermore, if you have a chance to livestream, livestream. Outside of taking a shit or making sweet love, you need to be ready for your close-up.

I know. I know. It sucks. But the more content you have, the more chances you have to get that content shared. And the more shares you get, the more you're on the radar or on the mind of potential voters.

It doesn't mean you have to be phony, nor does it mean you have to always be *on.* If you're having a bad day, show yourself having a bad day. Chances are, a good portion of your voters are also having a bad day. Hell, I did a video talking about having to carry an ass pillow with me to a morning show interview because my hemorrhoids had flared up. Aside from the dad jokes about it being a pain in the ass, people appreciated the realness.

Use the truths that are before you. You can't run out of honesty. Or at least that's what I told myself after realizing I had given a thirty minute speech on tax policy with a quite visible booger in my nose.

Nobody's perfect. And social media is a volume game. If you fuck up at 8am on Thursday, follow it up with enough share-worthy content that by 8pm everyone's already forgotten about it.

Is it fun being a tweet machine? Hell no. Is it fun taking thirteen gazillion photos for Instagram? Hell no. Is it fun doing videos for platforms you've never even heard of? Hell no. It was probably the worst part of the whole campaign. But what can you do? You can't pick the media era you wish to run in. You can only pick your nose before you go on stage. (Sorry, I couldn't help myself.)

One of the main reasons why proliferation of content is so important is name recognition. No matter how awesome your policies are, no matter how awesome *you* are, if people aren't familiar with your name, you ain't winning shit.

That's why we went as far as throwing a jingle contest. At risk of being seen as too cheesy, we gambled that the sheer name recognition this would garner us was worth it. Plus, we got hundreds of submissions, meaning there were hundreds of different jingles floating around the socialsphere, all hammering our name into voters' ears.

For instance, the one we picked didn't necessarily have the best lyrics, but the melody was so infectious we couldn't deny its earwormability.

"A Melody Is How You'll Remember" by Ruby Hoefle

There's simply no winning an election
unless you've got name recognition
but soon you'll know mine
with a jingle so fine
H.F. Valentine

Sure it's a gimmick Sure it's kind of hack
but we don't have a million dollar Super Pac
put it in a rhyme
works every time
H.F. Valentine

You may think it's silly, but without a doubt
once it's in your ear you'll never get it out
Melody is how we remember
Melody is how we remember
A melody is how you'll remember H.F. Valentine

The other valuable thing the jingle contest provided was a sizable amount of press. Not being able to rely on fair or even significant media coverage, sometimes we had to create the coverage. And as long as we stayed solid on our policy and fundraising integrity, I wasn't above a good old-fashioned publicity stunt.

In fact, we leaned into that shit. Early on in the campaign, we announced to the press that, for the publicity, I was going to pull off a literal stunt and jump a motorcycle over ten Rolls-Royces. Sure as hell, when the press showed up, I gave my statement in a red, white, and blue Evel Knievel ride suit. Except instead of giving a statement about the jump, I made an impassioned and articulate case to a half a dozen live rolling cameras as to why my campaign was worth taking seriously. When reporters asked me at the end where the Rolls-Royces were, I chided them for not seeing the obvious metaphor that I'd already made the jump by forgoing big dollar donations. Then, having held the event in the early evening, I jumped on my motorcycle and actually rode away into the sunset.

When my opponents pointed out how pathetic it was for us to resort to publicity stunts, we agreed. We agreed it was pathetic that the media had not previously given us even a fraction of the coverage my opponents had received. We agreed it was pathetic that my opponents were complaining about a publicity stunt whilst sitting upon industry-provided war chests.

We agreed it was pathetic for them to bring a gun to a knife fight and then cry when we dodged the bullets. A statement which actually gave us the idea for one of my favorite stunts of the race.

About midway through the primary, we held a press conference to thank all the rich assholes who had given to my opponents and not given to me. One by one, we identified big wig donors and their industry interest and expressed our sincerest gratitude for not placing the burden on us of owing them a favor once the election was over. We acknowledged that they could have given to anyone, and we appreciated them corrupting my opponents instead of me.

Similarly, while my opponents would announce their establishment political, media, and various other powerbroker endorsements, we would announce our establishment political, media, and various other powerbroker detractors. We would point out how those motherfuckers had been wrong on almost every issue and hadn't really done shit their whole career for anyone making less than six figures. I remember standing on the counter top of Rainey's Diner hollering, "For bootlickers and stooges to denounce us is all the endorsement we need. Their naysaying is my street cred. Their failure is my street cred. When they say fuck you, we say thank you!"

That's what it was all about. Not only was it good for publicity, but shit like that was what made the memories. We figured that if the odds were so far against us anyway, why not have fun with it? Do it your way. Don't be afraid to be tongue in cheek. Don't be afraid to let your slip show. Make it part of your mystique.

Whenever we were accused of a publicity stunt, we would own it. Bragging that at least we did our own stunts. Not like the CGI bullshit our big money opponents put in their movie. In a few years when their election story was collecting dust in the dollar bin at Walmart, our candidacy would be a cult fucking classic.

Our motto for the race was "Put the camp in campaign." And the only ones in on the joke with us were the voters.

Though as much as we relished fucking with the natural order of elections, we never lost sight of the gravity of our race. That gravity being the needs of the voters. Those needs were real. And each voter's need was a story.

I used to ask people to tell me their story on the campaign trail. Not to collect them for speech fodder, but to keep myself grounded to reality, their reality. I would tell them that I hear them. Then I would share with them why I believed the policy I was advocating for best met their need.

Of course, this wasn't my only use of storytelling. In the first two debates (before they caught on and quit playing along), I would ask my opponents to tell me a story, their own story, related to a certain policy issue. And if they couldn't, then I would tell them one of my own. And if they could, then I would explain in plain language why my policy addressed that story and why their policy, which was only theirs because it was approved by their donors, would only make that story worse.

And when I did engage in the obligatory storytelling on the stump, I was careful not to be fake with it. You can't exploit other people's stories or your own.

What you *can* do though is harness the power of our human connection. If you've never seen the "I have a story / I understand" part of Jesse Jackson's 1988 Democratic Convention speech, you need to put down this book and go watch it right now. It's one of the best utilizations of storytelling I've ever seen in the political realm.

As the old labor saying goes, there's power in a union. And that power is held together by a shared narrative. A story that everyone in the union understands, one that goes far beyond labor contracts and the logic of bargaining power. It's one of emotion. Of sadness and anger. Of compassion and love. That emotion is something we all share. And with every story I told on the campaign trail, I tried to build on our human connection, to extend that union.

Then again, it can't all be emotion. There has to be some real mechanism to bring about positive change. Often I would deliver speeches in three acts. I would start with emotion, then present the substance of my policy, then end with emotion. I called it the stump sandwich. And like a sandwich, the substance in the middle just doesn't seem right without some amount of emotion surrounding it. Yet without substance, without the logic and evidence behind the policy, the emotion is just empty calories.

Speaking of empty calories, if you're not setting the table for the day after the election, you're really just jacking yourself off. Barack Obama amassed an unprecedented organization of voters and volunteers, three million of whom had given their hard earned dollars toward his run, two million of whom were active members on the social arm of his campaign site, not to mention the 13 million email addresses stockpiled. Harnessing that army of hope could have resulted in the kind of change people truly expected. Instead, the day after inauguration he sent them all home and gifted whatever surplus value was leftover to the DNC. Eight years later, the Democrats had lost both houses of Congress, as well as countless state races, only then to suffer a humiliating defeat from one Donald J. Trump.

In a race like this, *you know* that every Republican that you can convince to vote for you has some serious expectations. Those expectations are born out of trust. Don't betray that trust. If you're going to make those connections, if you're going to gather those contacts, then you better do something meaningful with them.

If you win, you have a database to organize around your work in Congress. If you lose, you have a database to organize outside of DC politics. In both cases, you have the opportunity, and I would argue the duty, to organize people power. Moreover, you'd be galvanizing a mass of workers many on the left haven't even thought about organizing in years.

Assuredly, it will take a lengthy and concerted effort to do it right. But that's kind of what the fuck you're there to do. Running in a Republican primary as a lefty requires guerilla campaigning. And guerilla campaigning should, by nature, be a form of asymmetrical organizing.

That being said, it's not my place to dictate, or even form, the questions you have to ask of yourself. And I sure as hell don't have all the answers. In fact, I have a sizable mountain of misgivings regarding certain aspects of my own run for office.

While I think it positively mattered the amount of speeches I gave, and overall time I spent, on different aspects of the economy, I think the criticism that I sacrificed too much on other issues is a fair one.

Not that I didn't get to make my voice heard on these concerns, whether in the debates or in individual interview questions. I did. But the absence within these pages of longer excerpts from the stump on issues that are near and dear to my heart demonstrate a deficiency, no matter how unintentional, in my candidacy.

I should have given full speeches on Israel/Palestine, rural concerns, and transportation. I should have made campaign videos on surveillance, net neutrality, and international trade.

Part of this had to do with mere oversight; part of this had to do with not having enough time and resources; part of this had to do with not working hard enough. And part of it had to do with the inevitable reality that you're never going to be able to run a perfect campaign.

It doesn't mean you shouldn't try. But it also doesn't mean you didn't try.

Because I do care so much about these issues, I had a hard time coming to terms with my missteps. The only thing that saved me from forever gazing into the abyss of lefty guilt was the unmovable truth, that there was work to be done.

Indeed, the only reason I agreed to do this book was because there *is* so much work to be done. But with so much work to be done, there is so much history to be made. Whether it's by running your own race or being a campaign staffer/volunteer in someone else's, you can be a part of that history. You can be part of this story.

Mr. Fred Rogers once said, "When I was a boy and I would see scary things in the news, my mother would say to me, 'Look for the helpers. You will always find people who are helping.'"

That's all I did. And it's all I'm doing now.

Just looking for the helpers.

My name is H.F. Valentine, and I'm betting on you approving this message.

www.ingramcontent.com/pod-product-compliance
Ingram Content Group UK Ltd.
Pitfield, Milton Keynes, MK11 3LW, UK
UKHW021910190726
13853UKWH00002B/608